Waffen SS: the asphalt soldiers

Waffen SS:
the asphalt soldiers

John Keegan

Editor-in-Chief: Barrie Pitt
Art Director: Peter Dunbar

Military Consultant: Sir Basil Liddell Hart
Picture Editor: Bobby Hunt

Executive Editor: David Mason
Designer: Sarah Kingham
Special Drawings: John Batchelor
Cartographer: Richard Natkiel
Cover: Denis Piper
Research Assistant: Yvonne Marsh

Photographs for this book were especially selected from the following archives: from left to right pages 2-3
US National Archives; 7 Brian Davis; 8 Suddeutscher Verlag; 10-15 Ullstein; 16-17 US National Archives; 16 Ullstein;
17 Ullstein; 18-19 Sudd Verlag; 20 Ullstein; 22-27 Sudd Verlag; 29 Bundesarchiv/Sudd Verlag; 30-32 Sudd Verlag;
33 Ullstein; 35 Sudd Verlag; 36-37 Sado Opera Mundi; 38-41 Sudd Verlag; 46-47 Ullstein; 47-52 Sudd Verlag; 55 Ullstein;
56-59 US National Archives; 60 Sudd Verlag; 66-71 Brian Davis; 72 Imperial War Museum; 75 Sudd Verlag; 77 Ullstein;
78-79 US National Archives; 80-81 Sado Opera Mundi; 82 Sudd Verlag; 83 Ullstein; 84-87 US National Archives; 88-89
Ullstein; 89 IWM; 90-92 Ullstein, 94 Ullstein/Sado Opera Mundi; 95-97 IWM; 98-99 Ullstein; 101 Sudd Verlag/Ullstein;
102 Sudd Verlag; 105-107 Ullstein; 106 Sado Opera Mundi; 108-109 US National Archives; 110 Ullstein; 112-113 Sado
Opera Mundi; 114 Ullstein; 116 Sudd Verlag/Ullstein; 117 Sudd Verlag; 118 Ullstein/Sudd Verlag; 120 Sudd Verlag;
122-123 IWM; 126-128 Sudd Verlag; 129 Sado Opera Mundi; 130-131 Ullstein; 132 Sado Opera Mundi; 133 Sado Opera
Mundi/Ullstein; 134-135 Ullstein; 136 IWM;140-141 Sado Opera Mundi; 142 Ullstein; 144-145 Sudd Verlag; 146 Ullstein;
147 Brian Davis; 148-149 Ullstein; 152 Sudd Verlag; 154-155 Ullstein; front and back cover Brian Davis

Contents

A law unto themselves

Introduction by Barrie Pitt

During the summer of 1940, a young corporal serving with a British County regiment found himself with several thousand others in a German prison-camp in Upper Silesia. At the beginning this did not bother him as much as might be supposed, for the weather was warm and his captors, flushed with triumph, were disposed to treat British prisoners reasonably well; but winter came, and with it a rising anger in Teutonic breasts against the unfeeling islanders across the North Sea, who by their stubborn stupidity in not accepting the fact that they had been beaten in fair combat with German arms, condemned them all to the continued rigours of military life.

Prison-camp guards became less agreeable in their attitudes, food became much shorter, and the corporal soon decided that the life did not suit him. His first escape lasted for three days, his second for all of ten minutes, his third for nearly a fortnight. But on each occasion he learned a little more of the art of survival in difficult conditions, and his fourth escape, during the bitter winter of 1941, lasted nearly six weeks before he was seen and reported by two small Pomeranian children, recaptured by green-clad and shakoed police, subjected to some

robust and fairly expert manhandling and finally dragged through the main street of a small town and into the guard room of a barracks.

He had been disturbed by his treatment at the hands of the police, dismayed by the SS sign above the barrack gates and on the collars of the NCOs inside the guardroom, and appalled by the vehemence of the stream of abuse which greeted the party as, with a policeman on each side, he was marched into a well-appointed office in front of a young but obviously high officer of the Waffen SS.

The stream of abuse – of which the corporal could understand but one word in twenty – continued, but gradually it dawned upon him that he was not himself the object of the vituperation and it was the policemen, standing rigidly at his side, who were turning pale.

Eventually they were allowed to depart, visibly shaken; the young officer spat a final malediction at their backs, turned to the corporal and said in perfect English.

'I must apologise, my dear fellow, not only for the way those churls have behaved, but also for my own lack of hospitality. Do take a seat.'

He produced schnapps (with an

apology that it was not whisky) ordered food and tactfully suggested that the corporal might care for a bath and a change of clothing. Three days later – during which time the corporal had been treated as a guest of honour and never subjected to anything remotely resembling an interrogation – guards from his prison-camp arrived to take him back and his host bade him a regretful farewell. The corporal thanked him for his kindness.

'My dear fellow,' said the SS officer as they shook hands, 'had you been in Berlin and I in London, we might well have been now reversing roles.'

On his fifth escape, the corporal was successful in returning home, and caused considerable surprise wherever he went by his firm defence of the SS as a military formation with a high code of conduct and a chivalrous attitude to their enemies. This attitude engaged him in many bitter arguments, but as long as he remained in England his conviction did not waver.

But in 1943 he went briefly to Yugoslavia, in early 1944 he was parachuted into Northern Italy and he was in France not long after D-Day. In all three places he came across evidence that not all SS officers were as chivalrous as his acquaintance in Pomerania and as it happened he had occasion to visit Oradour. When later he heard of the massacre of American prisoners at Malmedy, he no longer felt it necessary to declare that such stories were propaganda.

As John Keegan has pointed out in this fascinating account of the formations which wore the double streak, other students of SS formations have suffered the same bewilderment as the corporal. How could troops who fought with such almost superhuman bravery, behave so cruelly and callously towards those who fell into their hands? They seemed to have none of that fellow-feeling for the fighting-man which occasionally humanised the battlefield when occupied solely by Wehrmacht and British or American troops and they certainly acted with stupifying ruthlessness towards civilians.

In the end they were to demonstrate contempt even for their creator, for when Hitler in one of his most demented moments cast a slur on the bravery of the Leibstandarte, the officers returned their decorations to him in a chamberpot!

They were indeed a law unto themselves.

Himmler's Empire

Hitler's Germany, lacking as it did any coherent philosophy or rational programme, expressed its aims chiefly through slogans and symbols. Of the two it was symbolism which worked the more powerfully on the public mind, an effect due to Hitler's skilful choice of both arrestingly novel and profoundly traditional themes to provide the imagery of his movement. His personal totem, the Swastika, was as strange as it was striking to the eyes of ordinary Germans. It was for these reasons that he selected it. But he appropriated others which, at one level or another, were deeply familiar and deeply cherished in the German lands. The black and silver cross, which recalled the Prussian Wars of Liberation and Unification against the two Napoleons, also stirred memories of the Teutonic Knights' crusades against the pagan Slavs. The oakleaf and the eagle struck an echo of vanished empires, one mediaeval, one Holy and Roman, the third still a vibrant memory, but all commanding territories far wider than those of the Weimar republic; and the same imperial echo was struck, in a different key, by the legionary banners carried at the party rallies.

Nor was it only to history that Hitler appealed through symbolism; it was also to folkmyth. The cottage styles affected by the party's women members hinted at a nostalgia – however spurious – for the rustic Germany of village legend, while the broad-bladed dagger worn by its men spoke of an older, darker Germany of forests and hunters. Most potent of all, evoking as it did that twilight world of ferocious gods and desperate heroes which so dangerously obsesses the German romantic imagination, were the Nordic runes of the SS.

The double lightning flash, in silver on black, sat incongruously on the collars of many who wore it in the heyday of Hitler's Germany – minor bureaucrats, agricultural research workers, genealogists, statisticians; less so on others – police officers, propagandists and counter-espionage agents, not at all on some – concentration camp guards and the killers of the extermination squads. For the SS, from simple origins, had become by the middle of the Second World War, an exceedingly complex organisation. It exercised, in the first place, supreme authority over the German police forces, civil, criminal and secret, both inside Germany and in the occupied areas; second, direct and almost wholly unfettered control over the concentration camp system, including the detention, labour and extermination camps; third, command of a large army, fourth, ownership of sizeable manufacturing properties; fifth, the function of resettling 'racial' Germans living outside the borders of the Reich and of the 'racial indoctrination' of the German people; and sixthly though not lastly, for it is impossible to tabulate all the activities of the SS, a powerful and growing influence within the Nazi party and many other sectors of German life, one index of which was the eagerness displayed by party and non-party functionaries to secure honorary SS rank.

The runic flash stood therefore for much that was worst in Nazi Germany – worse by far than anything of which the Nordic mythmakers had to tell – but it would be wrong to imply that because the SS administered the Nazi programme of terror and repression every SS man was necessarily the agent or accessary of racial murder. Many belonged only to the Allgemeine (General) SS, a voluntary though always exclusive branch of the organisation which performed no functions, except to provide a pool of recruits to the executive organs and to confer a certain inner-party prestige on those who succeeded in joining it. To this group must be added the 'honorary' officers of the SS, a miscellaneous collection of men whom Himmler wished to favour and which

included Ribbentrop, the Foreign Minister, Meissner, Hindenburg's and Hitler's Head of Chancellery, Keppler, Hitler's economic adviser, and many others of forgotten importance. Some of course had crimes to answer for in their proper roles, but not as SS men. And one must further exclude from culpability a large number of those employed in one or another of the branches of the SS bureaucracy. Much of the most terrible testimony at Nuremberg concerned the work of obscure officials who scarcely ever left their offices but a great deal of the work done at SS headquarters was purely routine and some, like much that went on in Himmler's orbit, purely crackpot. 'In one department of his foreign intelligence service a school of eager researchers studied such important matters as Rosicrucianism and Freemasonry, the symbolism of the suppression of the harp in Ulster, and the occult significance of Gothic pinnacles and top-hats at Eton. An explorer was sent to Tibet to discover traces of a pure Germanic race believed to preserve the ancient Nordic mysteries in those unvisited mountains, while throughout Europe excavators sought for relics of authentic German *Kultur*'. It would have been difficult to arraign such people as these before any war-crimes tribunal, on whatever basis it was constituted.

The SS was nevertheless indicted as a body at Nuremberg and a verdict of Guilty returned against it, its members, excluding that proportion who were compelled into its ranks, being declared a criminal group. And indeed once it had been decided to indict organisations as well as individuals, the outcome could scarcely have been different, for the evidence established without doubt that its 'aims and the means used for the accomplishment thereof' had included the commission of war crimes and crimes against humanity, had indeed included scarcely anything else.

An organisational chart of the SS

Left: Himmler congratulates SS ski champions.
Above: Himmler, Gruppenführer Karl Wolff and party dignitaries at Quedlinburg, 1938

at the height of its power might not seem to support that view. For it would show twelve different branches, all discharging disparate functions, several quite innocuous, but all of apparently equal standing. Such a chart is misleading – deliberately misleading, for Himmler purposely complicated the internal structure of his empire so that no one except he should fully understand its workings. There were in fact five key branches – RKFDV, RUSHA, VOMI, RSHA and WVHA – which between them were responsible for almost all the cruelties inflicted by Germany on the people of Europe during the Hitler years.

The RUSHA (*Rass-und-Siedlings Hauptamt*) had begun harmlessly enough as the SS marriage bureau, its duties being to authenticate the Aryan ancestry of would-be SS brides, while the VOMI (*Volksdeutsche Mittelstelle*) was charged originally with caring for the welfare of 'racial' Germans settled abroad. With the growth of Hitler's – and Himmler's – empire from 1938 onwards, however, both branches were called on to extend their operations, the two combining to organise an enormous programme of racial re-settlement. These activities, coordinated by a third office, the RKFDV, entailed the deporting of hundreds of thousands of nominally German east Europeans from their traditional homes, the expropriation and displacement of an equal and probably very much greater number of Slavs and the consignment of racially undesirable or unassignable types to forced labour, the concentration camps or extermination.

The concentration camps were in the charge of the WVHA (*Wirtschaft-und-Verwaltungs Hauptamt* – Economic and Administrative Main Office) and it is unnecessary to dilate on its activities, which resulted in the deaths of all but a handful of the millions committed into its keeping. Of those millions, the majority would originally have been arrested, or taken into 'protective custody' by one or other of the agencies of the RSHA (*Reichsicherheits Hauptamt* – Reich Main Security Office): the Gestapo and the *Kripo* (Criminal Police), acting in conjunction with the SD (*Sicherheitsdienst* – Security Service), originally the party's intelligence service, later that of the state. These three agencies did not however function merely as a police force. Each supplied drafts to the *Einsatzgruppen* (Task Groups) which, under the command of officials of the RSHA, did to death, usually by shooting or gassing, the majority of people exterminated outside concentration camps in eastern Europe during the war. The numbers run into hundreds of thousands and most were killed in a period of eighteen months in 1941–42. In the main they were Jews of the poorest class, settled in the great ghettoes of eastern Poland and western Russia, whither they had originally fled from Christian persecution in the 16th and 17th Centuries. Those Jews living more widely dispersed in the rest of occupied Europe were brought together for the 'final solution' by another, perhaps the most odious of RSHA sub-branches, Amt VI, directed by Adolf Eichmann.

The wording of the Nuremberg Tribunal's verdict on the SS reads, in the light of the testimony presented, surprisingly moderately. It found that the SS was 'utilised for purposes which were criminal under the Charter, involving the persecution and extermination of Jews, brutalities and killings in concentration camps, excesses in the administration of occupied territories, the administration of the slave labour programme and the mistreatment and murder of prisoners of war' and accordingly condemned it as a criminal group.

It was a judgement with which few Germans felt disposed to quarrel at the time, for 'even in Germany (the SS) inspired general fear and hate'. Nor in subsequent years has there been anything like a sustained attempt to rehabilitate the organisation. Individual SS men still find it politic to conceal their past and will continue to do so as long as the Federal German government keeps alive its investigation of war crimes, as well because of the odium as the penalty which exposure entails.

One branch of the SS however, in numbers by far the largest, was never prepared to accept that it merited condemnation and, with the passing of the years, has found the confidence and the voice not merely to deny the justices of the Nuremberg judgement but even to press its members' claims to compensation for the discrimination they have suffered as a result of it. That branch is the Waffen (or Armed) SS. Despite the fact that numbers of Waffen SS men, including several of their most prominent leaders, have been individually tried, sentenced and in some cases executed for war crimes committed in and out of the field, it is the argument of their former comrades that their acts – even if admitted – were in no way representative of the tasks which the Waffen SS was called upon to carry out; that those tasks

Himmler as Bavarian Police President, 1933

were, on the contrary, purely military in character; and that it is only by a perverse and wilful misunderstanding of the structure of the SS that the Waffen SS can be shown to have had links with the rest of the organisation. That the record of the Gestapo and SD dishonours the reputation of all SS men they will concede; but they will insist that theirs was a good name, dishonoured unthinkingly by the bureaucrats who originally designed the structure (they should of course really blame Himmler), subsequently and vindictively by the Allied judges.

The Waffen SS, their case runs, knew nothing of the concentration camps or extermination squads and would have recoiled in disgust if it had found out. Those Waffen SS men who had a hand in the work of terror and repression it portrays as interlopers – policemen, political appointees, criminals, or foreign volunteers – who would not have been accepted by the organisation in its founding years and should never have been allowed to wear its uniform. The field-commanders who shot prisoners or executed civilians are represented either as misfits, whom no army can avoid the mistake of recruiting in small numbers, or as casualties of the fearful strain under which Waffen SS units constantly operated.

For it is central to the argument of the veterans who seek to reverse the judgement of Nuremberg, that the Waffen SS was not only exclusively a military force but one called upon to bear the heaviest burdens in the most testing crises of the war. And, moreover, that it fought consistently harder and longer than units of comparable size in the same circumstances; that it was, in short, the élite strike arm of the Wehrmacht. To argue this case, it is necessary to omit from the list of Waffen SS formations a large number, perhaps the majority, of units which in theory belonged to it, and to deprive more than half of all the soldiers who wore the double lightning flash of the status of SS men. For the Waffen SS, like the larger organisation of which it formed part, was a heterogeneous body. It has been calculated that it numbered over fifteen nationalities on its strength, and nearly forty divisions on its order of battle, and that the total of men who passed through its ranks from beginning to end was over a million. A very high percentage of those became casualties, but a disproportionate number fell on a handful of the divisions committed; the remainder, and most of the men who belonged to them, therefore contributed little to the German war effort and figured very infrequently, if at all, on the major battlefields of the Second World War.

It is therefore to the achievements of an inner-core, the so-called élite or classic divisions of the Waffen SS, that the apologists and champions of the order turn in order to demonstrate its superiority in combat and the irreproachability of its behaviour. And those achievements were without argument impressive. The course of half a dozen major battles would undoubtedly have run quite differently had it not been for the intervention of Waffen SS corps and divisions, and at no place where they were committed, with or without a battle-winning mission, did they fail to heighten the intensity of the fighting.

That they did so their champions ascribe to two factors: to the very rigorous standards of selection imposed on volunteers and to their espousal of a particularly demanding creed of combat. The question of selection and of volunteering is, as we shall see, a complicated one. But the creed of the SS though more intangible, is also more straightforward. Its tenets have been summarized thus: that an SS man's basic attitude must be that of a fighter for fighting's sake; that he must be unquestioningly obedient and become emotionally hard; that he must have contempt for all 'racial inferiors' and, in lesser

Above left: Theodor Eicke, commander of the original concentration camp guards and later of the *Totenkopf division. Above right:* Adolf Eichmann, the SS expert on the 'Jewish question'. *Right:* Field-Marshal von Blomberg, Minister of War, chief victim of the SS plot against the army in 1938

measure, for those who did not belong to the order; that he must feel the strongest bonds of comradeship with those who did belong, particularly for his fellow-soldiers; and that he must think nothing impossible. It was in short, a superman's creed, and had deep roots in German thought. Treitschke and Nietzsche, the two most important philosophers of state power in 19th Century Germany would have subscribed to everything – at least in theory – which the SS creed taught and the latter might well have recognised, in the SS soldier, the embodiment of the superman to whom he gave literary existence.

'War is not only a practical necessity,' Treitschke wrote, 'it is also a theoretical necessity, an exigency of logic. The concept of the state implies the concept of war, for the essence of the state is power. That war should ever be banished from the world is a hope not only absurd, but profoundly immoral. It would involve the atrophy of many of the essential and sublime forces of the human soul.

A people which become attached to the chimerical hope of perpetual peace finishes irremediably by decaying in its proud isolation.' Nietzsche echoed these ideas in an even more direct exhortation. 'Ye shall love peace as a means to new war and the short peace more than the long. You I advise not to work but to fight. You I advise not to peace but to victory. Ye say it is the good cause which halloweth even war? I say unto you: it is the good war which halloweth every cause. War and courage have done more great things than charity.'

Nietzsche was even prepared to justify the most atrocious behaviour if undertaken in the spirit of the philosophy he propounded. 'The strong men, the masters, regain the pure conscience of a beast of prey; monsters filled with joy, they can return from a fearful succession of murder, arson, rape and torture with the same joy in their hearts, the same contentment in their souls, as if they had indulged in some students' rag. When a man is capable of com-

14

Above: The Stabwache in Berlin, 1933. *Below:* The Leibstandarte on parade at the Nuremberg Party Rally, 1935. *Right:* The Charlottenburg contingent of the General SS marching through Berlin

The Leibstandarte parade in celebration of Adolf Hitler's fifth anniversary as Führer. With him are Hess and Himmler

manding, when he is by nature a 'Master', when he is violent in act and gesture, of what importance are treaties to him? To judge morality properly, it must be replaced by two concepts borrowed from Zoology: the *taming* of a beast and the *breeding* of a species.'

The exculpation of the Waffen SS rests, of course, upon the argument that its soldiers, while selected by standards of which Nietzsche would have approved and inspired by the vision of war and of service to the warlike state and leader which he advanced, never descended to the actual level of behaviour he was prepared to justify in supermen; that the Waffen SS was, therefore, both aggressive and temperate in spirit, and that the virtues which it embodied, and which it was the object of its training to instil, were never perverted. It is again and again to the ideals of the 'original' SS that old Waffen SS men turn to illuminate their arguments. For those ideals,

they insist, were admirable and, whatever the misdeeds of the 'other' SS, were kept alive by the fighting branch in the greatest and fiercest battles of the war.

Is there anything in this argument? Was there an SS of brave and simple soldiers whom the torturers, in stolen uniforms, besmirched? Did it turn the tide of battle on a dozen stricken fields? Did its divisions still hold high their colours when others had struck theirs? That an SS army several hundred thousand strong existed and fought is a fact of history. But whether it was in any sense an army apart,

different in quality from the regular army, inspired by different and higher ideals, chosen by different and higher standards, are not questions to which any short or simple answer can be given. The Waffen SS was undoubtedly itself. But was it quite what it wanted or has subsequently claimed to be? Its cultivation of the virtue of loyalty, by which it meant unquestioning obedience, also meant that it could never be the master of its fate. If therefore one seeks to understand what the Waffen SS was, one must begin by uncovering the motives which impelled its leaders to raise it.

19

From the Putsch to the seizure of power

The origins of the SS are as obscure as those of the Nazi party itself, to which it belonged in spirit as closely as both to the times and the place into which they were born. The times were the early 1920s and the place Bavaria. And Bavaria in the early 1920s was a state racked by the recent memory and ever-present threat of violence. It was there that the revolution of 1918 had begun, with the deposition of the Wittelsbach King, and there that the revolution had taken its most violent turn. The socialist regime which succeeded the last royal government was itself quickly replaced by a communist republic and when it too was extinguished in a right-wing coup, carried out by troops of the regular army and the *Freikorps*, its adherents were executed in their hundreds. The socialists, whom the coup restored, were left in no doubt by those who had organised it, that they ruled only on sufferance. And that sufferance was withdrawn in March 1920 when the local army commander, taking advantage of the confusion spread by the Kapp *putsch* against the central Berlin government, removed them from office and set up in their place a thorough-going government of the right.

Henceforth it was the right which ruled in Bavaria and very much on its own terms, for the constitution of the Wiemar Republic allowed considerable autonomy to the governments of the states and one like the Bavarian, in any case the heir to a strong separatist tradition, could do much as it liked within its own borders. Since the central government was Social-Democrat in character and the Bavarian was not, the two were therefore generally out of sympathy and often at loggerheads. Nor was it only the elected members of the state government who were rightward inclined. So too were many of its civil

The SS guard Hindenberg, Hitler and Göring at Tannenberg Memorial Day, 1933

servants, of whom perhaps the most notorious was Pöhner, the Police President in Munich and Hitler's original protector, the man who, asked if he knew that there were political murder gangs in Bavaria, answered, 'Yes, but not enough of them'. Under the aegis of men like this, parties of the most extreme nationalist and separatist tinge flourished, maintaining their own paramilitary forces and attracting into the state the remnants of other *Freikorps* made unwelcome by the turn of events elsewhere in Germany.

The *Freikorps* – the name is self-explanatory – were a phenonemon which no account of post-imperial Germany and of the rise of Hilter can leave out of account. Raised as emergency units from among demobilised servicemen who remained true to the authoritarian creed of the old army, and used originally to expel the troops of the revolutionary councils from their citadels in Berlin, Munich and the other large German cities, they were quickly to become a second Reichswehr and eventually a power in their own right. But that last phase in their development came when their real usefulness had passed. As long as the army lacked the cohesion to deal with internal disorder, as during the years 1918-1919, or the right to intervene, as in the fighting between Poles and Germans over the disputed Silesian frontier in 1921, it was glad to equip, train and pay the *Freikorps*. Later their continued existence provided the army, whose strength had by then been fixed by the Allies at no more than one hundred thousand men, all to be enlisted on a twelve year engagement, with a welcome assurance of a partially-trained reserve. But once the army had come to terms with the Republic, in particular once it had established its power, in fact if not in law, to exercise ultimate authority in the state, then it quickly lost patience with the pretensions of the *Freikorps* to military privileges and a voice in national affairs.

21

The 'Oberland' Freikorps during the Bavarian Civil War, 1919

This change of face is in no sense surprising. For the hard-core members of the *Freikorps* – not the many who had taken up arms in defence of property and order during the worst months of the revolution, but the few who refused to lay them down even five years after the war had ended – had ceased to act or think as soldiers of the sort the generals understood. They had, as individuals, little to recommend them; had they been English, they would have found themselves most at home in the Black and Tans, if indeed they had not found that body too tame for them. Nor were all any longer true 'front fighters' of the sort who had fought the street battles with the Spartacists in the Berlin of 1918. Of the individuals and the units which, like Hitler's newly formed *Sturmabteilungen*, claimed membership of the *Freikorps* tradition,

many in 1923 belonged to it rather by wish than fact. What united them, and what also made them so repugnant to the generals, was the brute irrationality of their attitudes. They had never really accepted the reality of Germany's defeat in the field and everything that flowed from it – the loss of territory, the limitations of armaments, the Republic, democracy itself – they rejected absolutely. They had drawn their own conclusions, moreover, from the role which the *Freikorps* had played during the revolutionary crisis. And that was that force was not only the ultimate sanction in politics but that there were no limits to its usefulness. Thus, while the generals had recognised that neither the nation nor the Allies would tolerate a remilitarised Germany and, however distastefully, had accordingly made their peace with the Republic, the *Freikorps* persisted in believing that the sort of government they wanted – nationalist, authoritarian and revanchist – could be set up and maintained by armed force. Nor could they be persuaded that the army would not join them when and if events offered the opportunity to strike.

The bulk of the army stonily refused to lend any encouragement to this belief. Not so, however, in Bavaria. There it was not forgotten that the Bavarian army had until 1918 formed an autonomous contingent within the imperial forces, and the local command preserved like the Bavarian government, a strongly independent spirit in its dealings with Berlin. In the person of Crown Prince Rupert of Bavaria who was not merely heir to the toppled throne and the possessor of a distinguished military reputation but also, unlike the Kaiser, a resident in his former possessions, the Bavarian command had an alternative focus for its loyalties. It was indeed the Prince's continued popularity and presence which lent much of what substance there was to the issue of Bavarian Separatism. But separatism was not the only issue in Bavarian politics. Hitler himself, though as yet unknown outside Bavaria and merely one of several extremist politicians to lead minor parties within the state, had no time for a policy which set such limits on his ambitions. And while prepared even so to make common cause with the separatists in any movement designed to undermine the authority of the Social-Democrats, and their allies in Berlin, his difficulty was to find any cause in which the local government, extremist parties and para-military organisations could be united to oppose them. In the autumn of 1923, however, such an opportunity presented itself. Earlier in the year the French government had, in order to extract reparation payments on which Berlin was falling behind, occupied the Ruhr, and in protest the Berlin government had instituted a campaign of passive resistance against their troops. The campaign did not succeed, but its cessation though restoring normal relations with the Allies, provoked strong protests throughout Germany – so very strong in Bavaria, that the government there suspended the constitution on the pretext that open disorders would otherwise result, and appointed a commissioner with dictatorial powers.

Commissioner Kahr scarcely bothered to conceal that he looked forward to extending his dictatorial regime to the whole of Germany and when the Berlin government reacted by declaring a national state of emergency he refused to recognise its effectiveness. An open breach between the two governments was thereby made inevitable, though it was ultimately provoked by Kahr's rejections of Berlin's order to suppress Hitler's paper, the *Volkischer Beobachter* which persisted in vilifying the reputations of the leading figures in the Berlin government. The breach was widened by Berlin's attempt to relieve General von Lossow of the Bavarian command and made absolute by his swearing an oath of allegiance to the Bavarian government.

Kahr and Lossow next sought grounds and means to extend the conflict beyond the borders of Bavaria. The means lay ready to hand – in the *Freikorps* and party para-military forces which had made Bavaria their home and which Hitler's ally, Röhm, had recently succeeded in uniting into a *Kampfbund*. The grounds were provided by the action of the neighbouring state governments of Saxony and Thuringia in admitting communists to membership. Kahr's plan was to concentrate the *Kampfbund* on their borders and appeal over the heads of the Berlin government to German middle-class opinion, which would certainly support any purge he directed.

Neither Kahr nor Lossow was willing, however, to deal with the *Kampfbund* through Hitler, whose person and policies they distrusted, and while they manoeuvred to separate the *Kampfbund* from him, the

Above: Government troops attack Spartanists in Berlin, 1919
Below: Re-occupation of Berlin by government troops, February 1919

Above: Streetfighting, Berlin 1919. Below: 'We will fight them on the rooftops', Berlin, 1919

Berlin government itself struck against the two errant states. Kahr had thus mistimed his stroke; he had not, however misjudged his temporary ally's intentions. Hitler remained determined to challenge the authority of Berlin directly and on the night of 8th November, having assembled his own *Sturmabteilungen* and their fellows of the *Kampfbund* in and around Munich, siezed the *Burgersbraukeller* in which Kahr, with Lossow, was addressing their supporters, produced Ludendorff, the most prestigious patron of the extreme right, and declared a new Reich government.

These, the opening moments of the Munich *putsch*, were also its high point. During the course of the evening Hitler allowed Kahr and Lossow their liberty, which they used to re-establish their relations with Berlin and to prepare a counter-*putsch*, while he himself pressed on only in the most haphazard way with the consolidation of his own hold in the city. He secured few points of any importance – police headquarters and the telephone exchange, for example, were left unoccupied – and allowed the bulk of the *Kampfbund* to bivouac on the city outskirts. Next morning, when he at last recognised that he must move in force into the city centre, Lossow and Kahr had positioned police and soldiers to resist him. The humiliating climax of the march which followed is a well known story. Hitler himself dislocated a shoulder when falling or pulled to the ground at the first police volley, his followers fled leaderless and the small *Kampfbund* garrisons established in the city centre were dispersed or rounded up.

Hitler was to spend the next thirteen months in prison, a period of welcome respite in the politics of Bavaria. The authorities did not look forward to his release. 'The moment he is set free,' the Bavarian Police-President reported, 'Hitler will resume his political activities, and the hope of the nationalists and

racists that he will succeed in removing the present dissensions among the para-military troops will be fulfilled'. In fact, his fears were misplaced. It was true that the alliance of patriotic associations which had marched behind Hitler and Röhm at Munich fell quickly into disarray during his absence from the scene, as did the small Nazi party itself. But it was a disarray he lifted not a finger to check, was indeed content to let run its course. For Hitler, besides naturally fearing the emergence of a rival, had no interest in working to maintain the unity of a movement of which he was not visibly the head, the party being for him nothing but the vehicle of his all-devouring personal ambition. Moreover he was determined that he would never again resort to such crude and inchoate methods as he had used at Munich. The events of 8th-9th November 1923, had forced him to recognise that his belief in the army's benevolence was misfounded. It might not like the Republic but it liked its enemies even less and would shoot them down wherever and whenever they took up arms against it. He told one of his fellow prisoners at Landsberg, 'when I resume active work it will be necessary to pursue a new policy. Instead of working to achieve power by armed coup, we shall have to hold our noses and enter the Reichstag against the Catholic and Marxist deputies. If out-voting them takes longer than out-shooting them, at least the results will be guaranteed by their own constitution. Any lawful process is slow . . . Sooner or later we shall have a majority – and after that Germany'.

This 'path of legality', which Hitler was resolved henceforth to tread was not however one along which the para-military groups were inclined to follow him. Röhm, as leader of the *Sturmabteilungen* and architect of the

A Nazi presentation scroll for a former Freikorps fighter

Urkunde

Auf Grund der mir von dem Reichs-und Preußischen Minister des Innern erteilten Vollmacht beurkunde ich hiermit, daß der *Rittmeister Alfred Weser in Berlin*

an den Kämpfen des Freikorps

Maercker u. Ehrhardt

teilgenommen hat.

Es wird ihm hiermit Dank und Anerkennung des Reichs ausgesprochen, daß er freiwillig unter Einsatz von Leib und Leben das Deutsche Reich in schwerer Zeit verteidigt und geschützt hat.

Berlin, den 23. April 1936
Der Bundesführer
des Deutschen Reichskriegerbundes (Kyffhäuserbund) E.V.

S.S. Oberführer und Oberst a.D.

Kampfbund, remained true to the now demoded vision of maintaining his stormtroops as a secret Reichswehr against the day when it would join with the national army to overthrow the Republic and establish a dictatorship. The rank-and-file took a simpler but essentially similar view of the future and their determination to pass the time meanwhile in a round of marching, manoeuvring, beer-drinking, and political brawling filled Hitler with despair. Nevertheless he could not dispense with their services, in part because their numbers, which swelled quickly after the ban on the movement was lifted in 1926, provided the most impressive visual evidence of his growing strength, in part too because the use of violence, directed now not against the Republic but against his political opponents – Social-Democrats and Communists – remained an essential part of his strategy. Brawls at their meetings and street fights with their own ex-service leagues tainted their record, intimidated their followers and cast a steady drip of doubt on the ability of the Republic to maintain public order.

As Hitler well understood, however, the dangers he risked in running a mass para-military movement were immense. Should it get out of hand, the Berlin government might well use the excuse of its misbehaviour to suppress the Nazi organisation as a whole. Should it succeed too well in matching the army's cohesion and discipline, the generals, who knew and feared Röhm's ambitions, might well insist on its disbandment. Yet should Hitler, in his effort to steer it on a middle course, lay too heavy a hand on the tiller, the stormtroopers might turn and savage him. He was never satisfactorily to resolve these difficulties, not that is until on coming to power he rid himself of the need for mob support.

In the intervening years he dealt with the SA through a series of shifts and expedients. Immediately after his release, when it was the last danger which seemed to press hardest, due to Röhm's insistence on regarding the 'military' as the equal of the 'political' wing of the movement, he severed his connections with that very unpleasant man and appointed a more conventional ex-officer, Captain Pfeffer, to lead it. Pfeffer proving no more flexible in his view of the SA's role and good deal less effective in keeping it to heel, Hitler dismissed him in 1930 and persuaded Röhm, who had emigrated to Bolivia, to return and resume command. Röhm quickly reasserted firm control from the centre. But he was also instrumental in swelling its numbers – a trend to which the rising tide of post-depression unemployment contributed – and indirectly therefore in provoking an increase in the tally of murderous street-brawls with the communist fighting organisations.

In 1932 Hitler was consequently forced to acquiesce in a governmental decree for the SA's disbandment. Token though this disbandment was, Hitler's acquiescence was not wholly reluctant, for it was a measure of the SA's essential mindlessness that the growing probability of a Nazi victory at the polls drove it to precisely the sort of excess calculated to deter the hesitant voter. This arrogance showed itself in a growing impatience with party control. The Berlin section had twice mutinied between September 1930 and April 1931, the party offices in the city being reoccupied only with the help of the police. Even before the disbandment, therefore, Hitler was moving to the conclusion that the SA posed a threat not merely to his party's prospects but to his own authority, and had begun to think of means to counter it. What he needed was a compact, inner-party force, dedicated not to some vague and violent revolutionary creed, but to an unswearing loyalty to his own person. In the SS, led by the almost unknown Heinrich Himmler, he had the makings of just such a body of men. The separate identity of the SS

Above: Röhm, head of the SA and the German crown prince ('Little Willie')
Below: Sepp Dietrich (second from left) at Templehof airport with other SS leaders

Above: Crownprince Rupprecht of Bavaria reviews the 19th (Bavarian) regiment at Munich, December 1924. *Below:* Generals Brauchitsch (right) and Fritsch at his installation as honorary colonel of the 12th Artillery Regiment, 1938. This was the only gesture of restitution made by Hitler after his humiliation.

(*Schutz Staffeln* -Protection Squads) had been slow to emerge. Originally Hitler had relied for personal protection on a group known as the *Chauffeureska*, three or four professional toughs who took it in turns to drive his car. In preparation, for the Munich *putsch*, they had recruited a strong-arm band, known as the *Stosstruppe Hitler* (Shock Troop Hitler), whose title derived from that of the élite divisional assault groups which had spearheaded Germany's last desperate offensives in 1918. High-sounding though the title was, the group played an even less distinguished part in the *putsch* than most, its role being confined to destroying the printing-machinery of the local Social-Democrat newspaper. Nevertheless, Hitler on his release from prison reformed and renamed the *Stosstruppe* and arranged for the organisation of similar *Schutz Staffeln* in a number of other major cities in which he was likely to appear. Their purpose was to serve as his personal bodyguard, as and when needed, their numbers were kept accordingly small, twenty or so to each group, and their existence remained little known. In April 1929 there were in all no more than 280 SS men and there were no plans to add to their number. But that was also the month in which Hitler appointed Heinrich Himmler, an obscure party official, to take command of the organisation.

Himmler remains an enigma to all who knew him, and so deep an enigma to those who have tried to plumb his character at second-hand that he has been called a 'sphinx without a secret'. Meek to the point of servility in his dealings with Hitler, even when at the height of his power in 1944, amiable to his equals, understanding to his subordinates, kind to animals, unseeking in money matters, modest, even thrifty in his style of life, and rendered easily distraught by any display of physical cruelty, he discharged his functions of torturer and murderer without scruple, hesitation or pity, with a clear conscience and with his eyes open. Nothing in his early life hinted at the monstrous career he was to make for himself – for make it he did, without compulsion and despite the bitterly jealous opposition of the many competitors for power around Hitler's throne. The son of a modestly successful Bavarian school-master, and by all accounts a dutiful and affectionate son, the godson of a Bavarian prince whom his father had tutored, and therefore not unprivileged from birth, he may, as he claimed, or may not have seen action in the last year of the First World War but more probably spent his short period of military service as an officer cadet. On demobilisation, he returned to his studies, at which he did not shine, and qualified in 1922 as an agricultural chemist.

It was not a particularly promising start in life, his career did not prosper and, like many similarly untalented young men of the time, he took up the politics of the extreme right, which seemed to offer fulfilment of his deep need for personal recognition. He had probably served in one of the Bavarian *Freikorps* during the months of revolution and certainly took part, as a member of the *Reichkriegsflagge*, in the Munich *putsch*, an adventure which cost him his job. But it was after 1924 that his real political life began. He joined the Nazi party soon after Hitler's release and thenceforth devoted himself almost exclusively to party work, acting first as secretary to the Strassers, Hitler's rivals for the party leadership, then as Goebbel's assistant in the propaganda service. During this period he married a fellow-vegetarian and set up his chicken farm; both undertakings were to fail. It was also during this period that he became second-in-command of the SS having joined in 1925 with the number 168, and so found himself in 1929 next in line for the succession when Hitler decided to relieve Heiden, one of his original body-guards, of the leadership.

Left: **Himmler, Hitler, Göebbels and Göring in mufti, 1930.** *Above:* **Himmler and Blomberg, before the plot**

It is not clear what role Hitler had in mind for the SS or how, if at all, he intended that it should develop. Himmler from the first seems to have lacked all doubt. He could not, of course, foresee the range of functions which the SS was to acquire, since the majority were to fall to him piecemeal, but he was determined that it should become a decisive force in party affairs and that it should consist of a particular sort of German, the sort that he at face value was not. He was slight, sickly, myopic, squeamish and physically unprepossessing. His followers, of whom he already thought as Knights of a new German Order, were to a man to be triumphantly Nordic, tall, blond, robust, deep-chested, eagle-eyed, unfalteringly brave and unquestioningly loyal. The type he sought was of course an abstraction (of the sort which obsesses

the homosexual phantasist), and although he was to boast later that he accepted no-one for the original body-guard with as much as a filled tooth to mar his physical perfection, he could not and was never to find enough young Germans to people his dream. But it was by and with dreams and abstractions that Himmler lived and for him they possessed reality. Unlike Hitler, who lived only for power and had no time, though much private scorn, for the racial mythology of Nazism, Himmler had at some formative stage swallowed whole the claptrap theories of ethnic superiority and 'blood and soil' peddled by the Nazi thinkers, Rosenberg and Darré; and on them he continued to feed for the rest of his life.

The substance of these theories may be briefly summarised. Rosenberg believed that the Germanic peoples embodied unique qualities of hardihood and dynamism which entitled them to rule over their racially

33

different and hence inferior neighbours. Darré went on to argue from these assumptions that the superiority of the Germans was genetic, and that the 'gene bank' was held by the Nordic peasantry 'whose blood was as rich and fruitful as the soil they tilled. So great was their virtue that the future strength of Europe depended on the survival of their stock; it was essential that they should breed and multiply until their blond and shining youth outnumbered and outfaced the lurking decadent Slavs and Jews, whose blood was poison to the human race and whose haunts were the healthless streets of towns and cities'.

Darré's argument, in short, was for controlled inter-breeding and in the SS his most important convert, Himmler, had acquired precisely the sort of control group in which Darré's theories could be put to the test. Darré himself was soon recruited into the organisation as head of the Race and Settlement Office which at first principally concerned itself with research into the genealogy of would-be recruits. None could complete his probation until he had satisfied Darré's office that his ancestry, traced as far back as 1750, was free of any taint of Jewish, Slavonic or otherwise inferior blood. Should he wish to marry, his bride had to undergo a similar investigation, and also to prove that her family had no history of hereditary disease. SS engagements tended therefore to be long ones.

It was a measure of Himmler's obsession with heredity that he particularly welcomed as recruits representatives of the German aristocracy, among which the SS came to enjoy in its early days a reputation as the most socially 'possible' branch of the Nazi movement. Among the earliest notables to join were Prince von Waldeck - Pyrmont, Prince von Mecklenburg, Prince Lippe-Biesterfeld, Prince Hohenzollern-Sigmaringen, and the Archbishops of Brunswick and Freiburg. Later, with the foundation at Wewelsburg Castle of an SS centre modelled on the Master's house of the Teutonic Knights, he was to attempt to transform the higher ranks of the organisation into a new, though pagan, order of chivalry. He also eagerly accepted ex-officers of the armed services (regulations prevented serving officers from joining political organisations), news which brought in 1931 to the door of his chicken farm the most notorious of all his future subordinates, Reinhard Heydrich. Mistaking his previous post as a naval cypher officer for a counter-espionage appointment, Himmler immediately commissioned Heydrich to take charge of an inner-Party intelligence service, the *Sicherheitsdienst* (SD), which he intended to set up. The outcome of this impulsive decision, based exclusively upon the impression made on him by Heydrich's extraordinarily striking appearance, the quintessence of Aryanism, and cold ruthlessness of manner, was the creation in time of the secret police system and the extermination squads. That Himmler certainly did not foresee; but in matching man with job his instinct served him on this occasion uncannily well.

The majority of recruits to the SS in the two years before the Nazi seizure of power, however, rarely matched the physical standards which Heydrich personified, or indeed even the minima which SS regulations imposed, the selection procedures being inadequate to cope with the in-rush of those anxious to catch the tide while time allowed. Between January 1931 and January 1933, the SS grew from some 400 to over 50,000 members. Soon afterwards Himmler was to begin a weeding-out which sharply reduced these numbers, expelling many on grounds of physical or social inadequacy but also insisting on the renewed prosecution of genealogical

Crownprince Rupprecht and Prince Leopold of Bavaria as Field-Marshals

enquiries which sometimes caught out veteran SS men even after the outbreak of war.

This lack of discrimination, curious in an organisation which esteemed selection as a life-principle, is perhaps best explained in terms of the intense struggle for influence into which Himmler, probably but not necessarily prodded by Heydrich, threw himself during the period of 'the seizure of power' in early 1933, a struggle which not for the last time was to persuade him to accept numbers at the expense of quality. No doubt he made a pact with his conscience, which on this occasion he kept, but the compromise was nevertheless significant.

Manpower had suddenly become important to Himmler as a means to an end. He was not yet close to Hitler's inner circle and recognised as soon as

the 1933 election results were announced that if he were ever to establish a place for himself and his organisation in the Nazi scheme of things he had at once to secure an office of state from which to operate. That which he was initially allotted, the police-presidency of Munich, offered him little scope to enlarge his powers, certainly far less than Göring inherited through his appointment as Prussian Minister of the Interior, which conferred on him command of the Berlin police. The auxiliary force which Göring set up to extend Nazi control over the city, largely by terror methods, included 10,000 SS men and the man whom he appointed to oversee it, Daluege, was in fact an SS official; but he chose him in the knowledge that Daluege was his man, not Himmler's. Himmler and Heydrich had therefore to initiate a strategy of indirect approach, both being agreed that control of the police must be their immediate objective. The route they chose to follow lay via the political police authorities of the

From left to right: Milch, Fritsch, Mackensen, Blomberg, at the Potsdam Memorial Day for Frederick the Great, 1936

smaller states, most of which between April 1933 and April 1934 they succeeded in capturing. It was here that numbers counted, for Himmler's usual technique was to intimidate the city officials by a display of SS strength in the city and extract from them an invitation to assume police control. The procedure was as illegal as his methods, for the ultimate sanction over police appointments rested with Frick, the Reich Minister of the Interior. Himmler, however, simply failed to consult him and his injunctions always came too late to reverse events. In April 1933, Himmler felt ready to take on Göring and he set about the task in a manner which was to become familiar. At Göring's express displeasure, Heydrich had by then established an SD office in Berlin itself, to which he claimed had come information, undetected by Göring's own police, of a plot for his assassination. On the strength of it, Himmler successfully argued with Hitler the need to centralise control of the political police forces and was forth-

with appointed head of the Berlin Secret Police. This appointment, together with that he already held in Munich and the others he had appropriated in the smaller states, made him a man with whom the Nazi party and Germany would now have to reckon.

The extent of his organisation did not end there. Very shortly after his assumption of police powers in Munich he had set up, as many other local Nazi chiefs were doing, his own concentration camp. He located it at Dachau, close outside the city, and to staff it raised a body of *Totenkopf* (Death's Head) guards, recruited from among the SS and commanded by Theodor Eicke (later to lead the *Totenkopfdivision* in action). He had also found the means to establish for the first time a standing, armed SS unit, known as the *Stabwache* (Staff Guard) and commanded by Sepp Dietrich, one of Hitler's original bully boys. First stationed at the Munich Brown House, it was transferred in March 1933 to Berlin where, at Hitler's request, it took up the duties of nearest guard over the Reich Chancellery.

Provided, therefore, with his own intelligence unit which, under Heydrich, daily extended its surveillance over party, state and people, with control of the political police in the greater part of Germany, with his own prison system and with the nucleus of a private army in the *Stabwache* and the *Totenkopf* guards, Himmler had under his hand by the early summer of 1934 the makings of a comprehensive and extra-legal service of repression. He had succeeded in assembling it, moreover, at precisely the moment at which Hitler found himself in need of such an organisation. For the Führer's relations with the *Sturmabteilungen* and its leaders, so precariously preserved during seven years of waiting for power, had at last reached breaking point and he was bracing himself to implement the final solution of the *Freikorps* problem.

The SS, the SA and the army

By the beginning of 1934, the *Freikorps* were officially no more, Hitler having presided in Munich on the tenth anniversary of the *putsch* at their ceremonial disbandment, an occasion which included the laying-up of their colours in the Brown House, and his laying of a wreath on the tomb of their matyrs, inscribed 'Despite all, you have conquered'.

Outwardly, it was pure theatre, of the sort at which Hitler excelled and from which he drew deep satisfaction. Historically, it staked his claim to embody the traditions and spirit of the *Freikorps*. Politically, it settled nothing – for he least of all can have failed to notice that the guard of honour at the ceremony had been

found by the local contingent of the *Sturmabteilungen*. And within their ranks as he well knew and their chief, Röhm, would not let Germany forget, the destructive and irreconcilable spirit of the *Freikorps* lived on.

Had the seizure of power brought about a reduction or even a stabilisation in the size of the SA, Hitler could without risk have decided to disregard it as a factor in national affairs. But victory had, on the contrary, provoked a sudden and spectacular boom in its membership, which had risen from 300,000 in January 1933 to over 3,000,000 in December. This boom, a function of the economic slump whose contours the Nazi economic miracle had yet to erode, was more specifically the result of two developments: Röhm's wholesale incorporation into the SA of the nationalist ex-servicemen's leagues, the *Stahlhelm* and the *Kyffhauser Bund,* and the decision by hundreds of thousands of individuals to leap aboard the Nazi bandwaggon before it stopped rolling. Those who had leapt early enough and in the right spot had enjoyed a period of arbitrary and unbridled power, the Berlin SA having been given the freedom of the streets and the status of 'auxiliary' policemen for several weeks in the spring of 1933, during which they had paid off old scores and struck a satisfying chill of fear into the comfortable middle-classes. But the withdrawal of those privileges towards the end of 1933 and the over-crowding of their ranks with the unemployed and the opportunist, had implanted by reaction a bitter sense of frustration in the SA. Inherent in Hitler's message was a promise not only of national regeneration and international retribution but of socialist solutions to Germany's internal problems. And as the euphoria aroused by his triumph at the polls waned, so too did his followers'

Frank, Governor-general of Poland, reviews a Totenkopf unit near Cracow, 1940

willingness to await their rewards in patience.

The Nazi party was, in short, and despite its claims to indivisibility, rapidly dividing into a right and left wing, and the leaders of the left, impelled by the discontented mass of the SA, had began to talk of a 'Second Revolution'. Its objectives were vague, but economically were anti-capitalist enough to scare those powerful industrial and commercial interests which Hitler was now courting hard. More clearly stated, and therefore more disquieting, were its military objectives, to which Röhm was giving increasingly indiscreet voice. He had never foresworn his ambition to see the SA replace the Reichswehr, upon which he believed no truly national-socialist society could ever safely depend, and he insisted on behaving as the chief of the people's army of the future. The drift of this thinking and the flavour of his flamboyant personality is caught in the record of a conversation he had with Rauschning in early 1934.

'Adolf is a swine', he swore, 'he will give us all away. His old friends aren't good enough for him now. Getting matey with the East Prussian generals. They're his cronies now . . . Adolf knows exactly what I want. I've told him often enough. Not a second edition of the old imperial army. Are we revolutionaries or aren't we? . . . If we are, then something new must arise out of our élan, like the mass armies of the French Revolution. If we're not then we'll go to the dogs. We've got to produce something new, don't you see? A new discipline. A new principle or organisation. The generals are a lot of old fogeys. They never have a new idea . . . I'm the nucleus of the new army, don't you see that? Don't you understand that what's coming must be new, fresh and unused? The basis must be revolutionary. You can't inflate it afterwards. You only get the opportunity once to make something new and big that will help to lift the world off its hinges. But

Above: Reinhardt Heydrich, head of Reich security and incarnation of the SS type. *Right:* Hitler, Blomberg and SS guards, 1935

Hitler puts me off with fair words . . . He wants to inherit an army all ready and complete. He's going to let the 'experts' file away at it. When I hear that word I'm ready to explode. Afterwards he'll make National Socialists of them, he says. But first he leaves them to the Prussian generals. I don't know where he's going to get his revolutionary spirit from. They're the same old clods and they'll certainly lose the next war.'

Had Röhm had the discretion to restrict the expression of outbursts like these to his confidants, had he above all had the self-discipline to work by subterfuge and manoeuvre towards his ends instead of seeking to achieve them by threat and bluster, he might have come nearer their fulfilment. As it was, he contented himself with demanding – and receiving – a cabinet seat as Minister without Portfolio, from which he approached the Army High Command direct to enlist their support for the amalgamation of the two armies, his and theirs, under his leadership. The Army, already exercised by the unsettlement of its relations with the state which Hitler's accession to power had brought about, and in constant

SS Schütze wearing the M 44 pattern
blouse and trousers worn with canvas
gaiters over short black leather boots
The head-dress is the SS Burgmütze.
Worn attached to the black leather
belt are a pair of canvas M P 40 ammo
pouches. Stick grenades are stuffed
into the belt

SS Hauptscharführer from the
SS Totenkopf Division wearing 'autumn'
pattern camouflage smock and helmet
cover. Trousers tucked into marching
boots. Rifle ammo pouches are
supported by a set of black leather 'Y'
straps. A water bottle is hung from the
belt and entrenching tool just visible

negotiation with him over the form that relationship should take in the future, was now thrown into a fever of outrage and alarm at the open challenge to its status – as 'sole bearer of arms'. General Blomberg, the Minister of War, was able to parry it by an appeal to President Hindenburg, who rejected any such attack on the army's prerogatives. But the generals recognised that, Röhm's pretensions being what they were, this by no means quashed the danger for good, and they redoubled their vigilance.

It strengthened their hand with Hitler that others should have simultaneously taken fright at the SA's menacing posture. The western powers were known to disapprove strongly of its sudden increase in size, which threatened to nullify the limitations on military manpower imposed by the Versailles Treaty, and when Anthony Eden visited Berlin in February 1934 Hitler offered as his principal sop to foreign opinion, the promise of a two-thirds reduction in its numbers. But with or without allies, the army was in a commanding position over the SA question, for its good-will was crucial to Hitler's future. There was moreover a limit on the time he had available to win the generals' good-will, a limit all the more pressing for being undeterminable. It turned on the length of Hindenburg's life. The old field-marshal was now eighty-six and while he remained President, the army – which swore its oath of allegiance to him – remained outside Hitler's personal control. Hindenburg's death would offer Hitler the opportunity to succeed to ultimate power over army and state alike; but it would also offer the army the opportunity to throw its weight behind some other Presidential candidate. He had therefore to assure himself of the generals' support at the earliest possible moment. He knew that he enjoyed their confidence to an extent, for they had held their hands when they might have opposed him for the Chancellorship. They had also

shown their willingness to participate in the spirit of the new regime by their making of such concessions as the adoption of the party insignia as part of the military uniform. But he also knew that to guarantee himself the Presidency he would have to make concessions on his side, and that they would most probably concern the status of the SA.

Whether Hitler did or did not, aboard the cruiser *Deutschland* during the Baltic naval manoeuvres of April, conclude with Blomberg and Fritsch, the Army Commander-in-Chief, a pact which guaranteed him their support for the Presidential succession in return for his promise to suppress the SA is now disputed by historians. It seems in balance unlikely. It is known, on the other hand, that the generals kept up an unrelenting pressure on him to settle the issue, while making it clear that they would not permit him to use their soldiers if it came to blows – to that extent, maintaining their 'above party' tradition. Fortunately for Hitler, a strong shift of opinion against the SA was making itself felt within his entourage. Röhm's personal depravity, tolerated as long as the party was in opposition, had become distasteful to many now that power had come their way, while others, of whom Göring was the most important, envied and feared the weight of his following. Himmler, of course, regarded Röhm as his principal rival and it was symptomatic of the opportunism which characterised inner party affairs that he and Göring, so recently at loggerheads themselves, should by the spring of 1934 have determined to make common cause against their enemy. To this cynical friendship Göring brought influence with Hitler, Himmler a finely-tuned intelligence service – between them they set out to collect – and when collection failed, to invent – information harmful to Röhm and feed it into Hitler's ear. He, ever fearful of a counter *putsch*, listened readily, even if he did not immediately display

SS Untersturmführer wearing the old style Feldmütze and with the grass pattern camouflage smock rolled up for comfort and worn over the field-service tunic and service breeches with officers high boots. Around his neck are hung binoculars and he is holding a M P 40

SS Hauptsturmführer from the Leibstandarte SS 'Adolf Hitler' Panzer Division and Knight Cross Holder wearing a short cross over black Panzer uniform with trousers gathered at the ankles and short black boots. Head-dress is the officers 'Feldmütze'. Map case and pistol holster are shown

SS Unterscharführer wearing the field grey uniform for self-propelled artillery gun crews. Steel helmet and canvas gaiters over short boots complete the outfit. Decorations shown are Iron Cross 1st Class and Iron Cross 2nd Class ribbon

credence in the news he got. Early in June, he held a long private interview with Röhm, presumably in a last attempt to wean him away from his commitment to the 'Second Revolution' and parted from him amicably enough to be able to order, apparently without fearing a reaction, that the SA should spend the month of July on leave. Whether or not he had already made up his mind to strike against its leaders while their men were dispersed is unclear, but it is certain that Göring and Himmler redoubled their efforts during the following three weeks to convince him of the danger in which he stood.

His sense of insecurity was further heightened by a speech of von Papen, the nationalist politician whom Hindenburg had foisted on him as a watch-dog Vice-Chancellor, which, delivered on 17th June, attacked the regime in forthright terms. Angry though it made him, it also served him warning that time was running out. The same message was brought him by Goebbels, Röhm's last remaining ally in the inner-party, who had now decided to change his allegiance and to add his own reports of Röhm's untrustworthiness to the others. It was he who fabricated the news that the Berlin SA had been given orders to return to duty on 29th June, and it was this lie that proved decisive. Hitler, torn by indecision for a fortnight, now determined to act. How and against whom was settled for him by Göring and Himmler who had spent some weeks preparing plans for the purge, selecting those to be executed, keeping track of their movements and nominating their killers.

The total of deaths inflicted during the Blood Purge of 30th June (the Night of the Long Knives as it was soon to be called abroad, though the killings extended over two days) has never been accurately reckoned. Hitler himself, justifying his actions to the Reichstag three weeks later, admitted to fifty-eight; a more probable figure is about 400; some estimates run as high as 2,000. Whatever the number of victims, it included not only those whom Hitler himself had reasons, good or bad, to fear, like Röhm (surprised in bed with one of his SA men) and Strasser, his old rival, but also many of Göring's and Himmler's own enemies and at least one complete innocent, a Hamburg music critic who happened to bear the same name as the city's SA commandant. It also included two generals, Schleicher, the ex-Chancellor who had miscalculatingly helped Hitler to power, and Bredow, his military assistant. These murders did not please the High Command which, though feeling little regret at Schleicher's demise, naturally regarded its manner as setting a dangerous precedent. In general, however, the results of the Blood Purge so suited the army's book that, although its leaders had almost certainly not connived with the plotters, the suspicion still lingers that they may have done so.

It was a particular source of satisfaction to the army that the programme of wholesale shootings had been carried through without involving any of their own men. The execution squads had been found from the local police forces or, more often, from SS units and, after an initial display of alarm, the rank and file of the SA had accepted the attack on their leaders with remarkable docility. Search operations subsequently revealed, to the army's satisfaction, how great was the danger of civil war the country had been spared, for over 177,000 rifles, nearly twice as many as it possessed in its own armouries, were removed from SA centres. Once again, therefore, the army seemed to have pulled off the trick it had worked throughout the Weimar years: that of retaining ultimate power in the state without intervening directly in its affairs. It is measure of its relief that Blomberg should have expressed the army's thanks to Hitler, in an order of the

Above: Göring at Nuremberg, 1938, surrounded by SA and SS contingents
Right: Brauchitsch, the army commander, reviews Berlin SA, 1939

day of 1st July in these over fulsome terms. 'The Führer has personally attacked and wiped out the mutineers and traitors with soldierly decision and exemplary courage. The *Wehrmacht*, as the sole bearer of arms within the Reich, remains aloof from internal political conflict but pledges anew its devotion and fidelity. The Führer asks us to establish cordial relations with the new SA. This we shall joyfully endeavour to do in the belief that we serve a common ideal'.

The 'new SA' proved to be a shadow of its former self. Denied for good any prospect of supplanting the official army, it soon declined into little more than a Nazi old comrades' association, called out, if at all, merely for route lining duties on ceremonial occasions. Its numbers

too soon dwindled as the Nazi economic miracle found work for the millions who had crowded into it during 1933. Thus, as the army had hoped and worked for, the most immediate of the dangers raised by Hitler's accession was dissipated at a single blow.

But Hitler was now free to claim his side of their bargain, and on 1st August President Hindenburg died. On the same day, with reference to no one but in the belief that the army would abide by its unwritten agreement and with the determination to allow them no time for second thoughts, Hitler announced the fusion of the offices of President and Chancellor. On 2nd August he accepted oaths of allegiance, unconditional and personal, from the heads of the armed services and arranged for the same formula to be sworn by every soldier and sailor in Germany. They were now his men; but he, their leaders comforted themselves by believing, was still their client.

What the generals had not reckoned with, and did not yet recognise, was the emergence in the SS, of a new and potentially far more dangerous rival than the SA. That it was better-led and organised was dangerous enough; that the army should, in effect, have allowed it to wage a miniature civil war on the army's behalf was disastrous, abrogating as it did its jealously guarded right to be the 'sole bearer of arms' and its simon-pure principle of remaining above party. Yet the signs of the growing threat were there if they had been looked for. Hitler had already singled out for distinction Himmler's pet unit, the *Stabwache*, by conferring on it the title of *Leibstandarte Adolf Hitler*, at the Nuremberg Rally of September 1933. In November its members had sworn him an oath even more binding than that laid on the Wehrmacht after Hindenburg's death (it read: 'I swear to you, Adolf Hitler, as Führer, and Reich Chan-

The Leibstandarte at drill, 1938

Above: Start of the 3000 metres, SS athletic meeting. *Left:* Dedication of the Essen memorial to the Freikorps, 1934

cellor, loyalty and bravery. I vow to you, and to those you have named to command me, obedience unto death, so help me God'.) Hitler had thus already set up a body of armed men answerable to himself alone – a quite unconstitutional act – and without attracting a murmur of protest from the generals. In the aftermath of the Blood Purge, he carried this special treatment a stage further, announcing on 26th July that, 'in consideration of the very meritorious service of the SS, especially in connection with the events of 30th June, 1934, I elevate it to the status of an independent organisation within the National Socialist Worker's Party.

Thus was the first of Himmler's ambitions consummated. He was now a leader in his own right. But the leader of quite what remained undetermined. As unofficial (soon to be official) Nazi police chief, he had power, and power of growing dimensions, but that did not satisfy his craving for status. For status, in his very Germanic mind, was bound up with military rank. Hitler was now titular Commander-in-Chief, Göring a general. Himmler wished for command of troops of his own. And not merely of a token force. Impressive though the bearing of the *Leibstandarte* was, its strength by the end of 1934 did not exceed that of a regiment, while of the *Totenkopfverbände* it was impolitic to speak. He began to urge on Hitler therefore the necessity to enlarge this peculiarly trustworthy force, urgings which Hitler was not unwilling to heed in view of his continuing suspicions of the general's fundamental loyalty. He recognised, on the other hand, that the surest way to trouble that loyalty was to recreate the spectre of an alternative, – a party – army. The solution at which he eventually arrived demonstrated his uncanny skill in playing on men's greed at the expense of their prudence, for it linked the expansion of the SS to a very much more extensive expansion of the army as a whole. In his announcement of the plan to re-introduce conscription in March, 1935, he included notice of his intention to raise a divisional sized SS unit, to be known as the *Verfugungstruppe* (Reserve Force).

The creation of the *Verfugungstruppe* marks the institution of a formal distinction between the militarised SS and the rest of the organisation. For although the purpose of the new force was left obscure – its cost, for example, was to be a charge in the Reich police budget though it was not to perform regular police duty – it was clearly meant to be different in character from that other armed body of SS men, the *Totenkopfverbände*. They continued to

be concerned with the staffing and guarding of the concentration camps and were not drawn upon to provide recruits for the *Verfugungstruppe*. Its new units were raised instead by the bringing together of the isolated SS battalions, themselves the descendants of the 'Political Purpose Squads' set up in major German cities during early 1933, into two regiments (*Standarten*), *Deutschland,* stationed in Munich and *Germania,* stationed in Hamburg. The third regiment (all were of three battalions) was the *Leibstandarte,* stationed as before in Berlin. Despite its incorporation into the *Verfugungstruppe,* it retained a measure of autonomy, due to the old friendship of its commander, Sepp Dietrich, with Hitler. He, moreover, had been promoted major-general on the day of the Blood Purge and so outranked his nominal chief, Paul Hausser.

Hausser, whom Himmler had appointed to command the *Verfugungstruppe,* was well matched to the job. One of the few ex-officers of high rank to have joined the SS (he had returned from the Army in 1932 as a Lieutenant-General), he held strong views on the applicability of the 'soldierly virtues' to political movements and had been a natural choice to command the first SS cadets training centre (*Junkerschule*) set up by Himmler at Bad Tolz in Bavaria in 1935. There and at the *Junkerschule* in Brunswick, which he next directed, the future officers of the SS were put through perhaps the most rigorous and comprehensive leadership course ever designed. Reveille at six was followed by an hour's physical training, breakfast of porridge and mineral water (both SS proprietary brands) and a morning of weapon training and exercises. Three times a week the cadets received 'ideological instruction', at first from specially appointed instructors, later, when they seemed to

be developing what Himmler called 'commissar status', from the company officers. The texts most frequently used were Rosenberg's *Myth of the Twentieth Century* and Darré's *Blood and Soil.* The afternoon was spent on the square or the sports field, athletic prowess being highly valued. Indeed in that respect, the SS came to resemble the British far more than the German army, sporting achievement forming a powerful bond between officers and men. At a later stage in their training, SS cadets took part in live-firing manoeuvres, a notable innovation, and even, it is said, underwent such bizarre tests of nerve as that in which the initiate balanced a grenade, from which he had pulled the pin, on the top of his helmet and stood at attention to await the explosion. Whatever the truth of this story, the course undoubtedly produced dedicated and hardened young leaders. Whether they were of the same all-round quality as those produced by the army cadet schools is more doubtful, Himmler laying such emphasis on physical, racial and political selection that the minimum educational qualification had drastically to be reduced to secure adequate numbers. Before 1938 some forty per cent of the entrants had in consequence no more than elementary school education. The middle and upper ranks in addition were often filled by the 'old fighter' type, leavened with retired regulars who alone possessed real professional skills. Later, however, the rigours of war were to bring to the front a generation of young SS colonels and generals whose powers of leadership were perhaps unmatched in the German army.

Why a force still as yet dependent on the Ministry of the Interior for funds needed such intensive training for war was a question which neither Hitler nor Himmler would answer squarely before 1938. In private, however, both let it be known that its principal task was to act as the guarantor of the regime, as it had done

Göring and Himmler exchange insincerities, Nuremberg, 1937

in 1934. Himmler of course chafed at these limitations on its role. More discreetly than Röhm had done, he was already speaking of the need to replace the tradionalist army with a more politically committed force. But as he well knew this programme (which he was never to fulfil) could not even be hinted at while the army retained that measure of autonomy which had been its half of the bargain struck over the Presidency. Until its independence was broken, therefore, the *Verfugungstruppe* must remain merely an armed police, outwardly military but without true military functions or the opportunity to enhance its military efficiency.

But in January 1938 the opportunity to break the army's independence suddenly presented itself. Blomberg, the Minister of War, had recently married again and Heydrich was able to show that his bride had a record of prostitution. He was forced into retirement, leaving vacant the post which conferred direct authority over the Wehrmacht. His natural successor was the Army Commander, General von Fritsch, but against him too Heydrich's SD had been preparing a dossier. An informant was found who was prepared to accuse him of homosexual practices and although he later admitted that he had mistaken the general for a retired captain of the same name, Hitler had by then placed Fritsch on indefinite leave. Before the army could move to secure his reinstatement, Hitler announced that he intended to abolish the Ministry of War, vesting its powers in a joint Defence Command (OKW) of which he would assume direction. The individual services were left their own professional commanders, Fritsch being replaced by General Brauchitsch, but Hitler, now executive as well as titular Commander-in-Chief, was entitled to nominate their successors and to intervene directly in service affairs.

One of the first ways in which he chose to do so was by tackling the issue of the armed SS. It had now taken part in both the bloodless military operations with which he had opened his programme of territorial aggrandisement, the reoccupation of the Rhineland and the *Anschluss* with Austria. In the former the *Leibstandarte* had indeed been the first unit to enter the demilitarised zone. The *Verfugungstruppe* had also grown in size, the Austrian clandestine SS having been formed after the *Anschluss* into a fourth *Standarte*, *Der Führer*, which was stationed at Vienna and Klagenfurt. In August 1938 he therefore decided to specify in detail what its future functions were to be and what form its relations with the Wehrmacht should take.

The top-secret document in which he did so, affirmed again that the SS was a political organisation which for normal purposes need not be armed. However, and this announced an important policy departure, the *Verfugungstruppe*, *Junkerschule* and *Totenkopfverbände* were 'for special internal political tasks or for use with the wartime army' to be armed, trained and organised as military units. In war, these units were to come under the tactical control of the local army commander. The Reichsführer SS was, however, to remain responsible for their recruitment and internal administration and for their control in peacetime – as he was also if the armed SS was detailed for wartime duty within the Reich. Ultimate authority over their deployment was to rest of course with Hitler.

The document also dealt with what, for the army, was the most delicate question of all: in which units of the SS was enlistment to count as fulfilment of the obligation to perform military service? Hitler laid down that it would do so only in the *Verfugungstruppe*, in which terms of service were so rigorous that the army's call on the manpower pool was scarcely affected. Officers were enlisted for

Army, SS and SA on parade, 1933

The Leibstandarte route marching, 1936

twenty-five years, NCOs for twelve and privates for four. Enlistment in the *Totenkopfverbände*, now consisting of twelve battalions, was not to count as discharging the military obligation, though in war the battalions were to be mobilised as a special police force under the Reichsführer SS, and to be replaced in the concentration camps by older general SS reservists. To mark the assignment of the armed SS to military duties in the field, it was to adopt the

army's field grey uniform, though it was to retain its own peculiar badges of rank and collar runes and to wear its black for ceremonial.

This Führer decree, entitling the SS though it did to a place on the mobilised strength, seems to have been received by the army without demur, perhaps because of the rights of tactical control and peacetime supervision of training that it assured the generals, more probably because they were fully engaged in the rearmament and expansion of the Wehrmacht. Whatever the cause, little was heard

in the year which preceded the outbreak of war of serious differences between the two. Indeed in June 1939, General von Brauchitsch, the army's new commander, ordered that it should seek to develop 'a mutual relationship of trust and comradeship . . . which is the prerequisite for partnership in battle' and that local SS units should be invited to take part in training periods, courses, sporting events and social occasions run by the army. By that time, as a result of the *Verfugungstruppe's* participation in the annexation of the Czech Sudeten-land, of its growing military efficiency and of a highly realistic battle simulation that it carried out before Hitler himself, he had agreed to allow its transformation into a full field division. All that was needed to complete its table of organisation was an artillery *Standarte*, which was quickly formed, and some minor ancillary units. On mobilisation in September 1939, therefore the *Verfugungstruppe* already represented the nucleus of a major military force. Whether that nucleus was to grow would depend chiefly upon its performance in battle.

Blitzkrieg in the west

The campaign against Poland was a fair test neither of the Wehrmacht's capabilities nor of the *Verfugungdivision's* readiness for battle. Outnumbered and underequipped, the Polish army was overwhelmed in eighteen days of fluid and fast-moving fighting in which its patriotism and élan counted for little against Hitler's tanks and aeroplanes.

Inevitably the small size of the SS contingent denied it any prominent role in the German operations, and its contribution was the more easily overlooked because it was not even allowed to fight as a division. *Standarte Deutschland*, the artillery *Standarte* and the armoured reconnaissance battalion were brigaded with army units, *Standarte Germania* was attached to Fourteenth Army in East Prussia, and *Leibstandarte* was deployed separately in Silesia. *Standarte Der Führer* which belonged to *Leibstandarte* did not take part. None of those that did take part performed outstandingly, their casualties being disproportionate to their achievements, the result in the army's view of unskilful leadership, in Himmler's,

SS troops in Greece 1941. The mottled camouflage clothing was peculiar to the Waffen SS

Above: Hitler reviews the Leibstandarte, April 1940. *Below:* Himmler, Sepp Dietrich and Peiper review the Leibstandarte at the presentation of Hitler's personal standard to the regiment, September 1940

of a failure by the army to provide fire support.

Whatever the force of the army's argument, Himmler won permission from Hitler immediately after the close of the campaign to increase the number of SS divisions from one to three, and to the task of raising these new formations he devoted much of his energy during the months of *Sitzkrieg*. They were to be difficult months for he encountered many restrictions in his freedom to recruit, some imposed by his own strict code of selection, but most by the army which had in the Reich conscription laws a powerful weapon to thwart his efforts. Those laws laid down that no German of military urge could join the armed services until the local military registrar had given him clearance, a process which was governed by an adjudication between the manpower demands of the three branches, army, navy and air force. The proportion of recruits each was allotted fell roughly into the ratio 66:9:25, no special provision being made for the SS. While the SS was free therefore to solicit volunteers, it could give them no assurance, even if they met its standards, that they would eventually secure a posting. That would depend upon the Wehrmacht's goodwill and they strictly rationed the SS to no more recruits than would fill out its prescribed divisional strength. The announcement of the raising of its two new divisions won from the Wehrmacht grudging approval for the release of the necessary quota of volunteers from the manpower pool, but raw lads of eighteen to twenty were of no use to a man in a hurry, like Himmler. He needed trained men immediately if his new divisions were to take the field in a campaign which would certainly not be delayed later than the spring.

The solution which he hit on is an illuminating demonstration of his skill in manipulating administrative machinery, and of his readiness to compromise with his conscience. Reluctant to turn away the flood of teenage applicants which a nation-wide recruiting campaign had brought in, he formed for each division a replacement cadre which could hold them until they were trained. To fill out the skeleton of his new divisions meanwhile, he decided on wholesale embodiment of formations of the *Totenkopfverbände* and of the German civil police. The incorporation of the former, who were of course not strictly soldiers at all, was made possible by legal loopholes in the Führer's decree of 1938. These allowed him to call up older men on the outbreak of war to replace the permanent units of concentration camp guards. Those units, in particular *Totenkopf-standarten* 1, 2 and 3 were drafted into the second of his new divisions (henceforth known as *Totenkopf*) and were replaced by newly formed units of volunteers. Hence he created a reserve pool for his field divisions, and one over which the Wehrmacht could exercise no control. The formation of the third division was made possible by his decision to suspend the voluntary principle in its case. Thus it was that some thousands of constables suddenly found themselves in field grey and faced with a programme of training which, for many, was overtaxing to men of their years. As a result this division, *Polizei*, remained for long something of a second class unit.

With Poland conquered and Slovakia subjected, a third solution to the manpower problem, and one which in the long run was to prove the most effective, offered itself to Himmler and to his chief of recruiting, Gottlob Berger. This was to enlist volunteers from among the Polish and Slovakian *Volksdeutsche*, those German speaking communities which the Nazis chose to regard as citizens of the Greater Reich and whose existence justified in their view the enlargement of Germany's frontiers to include their homelands. The history of the *Volksdeutsche* under Nazi rule was to be as unhappy as almost any other of the peoples of Europe, treated as they were to be as pawns of Nazi racial policy, but in 1940 the programme of displacement and resettlement which they were to undergo had not yet begun in earnest. Their future under German rule looked bright and their young men volunteered for the SS enthusiastically. They were as enthusiastically accepted, for German though the Nazi leaders insisted that they were, the German state did not yet regard them so and had no means therefore to conscript them into the Wehrmacht. The SS was therefore free to recruit as many as it could find without any interference by the army. Their members were still insufficient to provide sizeable contingents but the principle was a promising one.

Himmler had less success with another attempt at individual enterprise in the military field, direct negotiation with the armament factories to equip his new formations. As soon as his approaches to the German Armaments Minister, Fritz Todt, were detected by the army (the deal was to entail the exchange of munitions and weapons against the transport of 20,000 Polish workers) it intervened to impede them. Hitler was brought to agree that contracts must be completed through official channels, and the SS was accordingly thrown back on the generosity of the Wehrmacht. As the Wehrmacht itself was pressed to outfit its new formations, this generosity proved grudging and although the *Verfugungsdivision* was fully equipped and motorised with the best of German weapons by the spring of 1940 and the *Leibstandarte* if anything oversupplied, *Totenkopf* and *Polizei* had to make do with requisitioned Czech armaments. For *Totenkopf* these at least included a full complement of motor vehicles, which put it among the handful of fully mobile divisions in the German armed forces. *Polizei* remained a marching unit, whose transport and artillery, like that of the bulk of the Wehrmacht,

was horsedrawn.

The last but in many ways the most important development undergone by the armed SS during the months of preparation between the battles of Poland and France, was an organisational one. Its leaders had not relaxed their efforts to have its status and composition established on a firmer foundation and in March 1940, they achieved much of what they wanted. Hitler then agreed that service in the *Totenkopfverbände* should count as military duty, thus affecting an important increase in Himmler's reserve of reinforcements for the field divisions, and he also announced that these two branches of the armed SS together with the cadet schools, the divisional reserve and training units and the administrative sections directly concerned should collectively bear the title Waffen SS. It was of course under this title that the armed SS was to become known, and feared, during the Second World War.

The campaign in which it was first to make its mark was now at hand. After repeated postponements, brought about by the German generals' fear of embroiling themselves in a war of attrition and later by their failure to submit a convincing plan of operations, the attack on France and the Low Countries was by April 1940 in the last stages of preparation. It was to take the form of a deep armoured penetration of the allied front at the point where the Maginot Line petered out south of the Ardennes forest, coupled with a diversionary offensive into Holland and Belgium. The object was to reach the sea midway between Calais and Le Havre, thus cutting the Allied armies into two, and subsequently to destroy each in detail. Army Group A, which was to make the central thrust, had accordingly been allotted the bulk of Germany's ten panzer divisions. The role of Army Group B in Holland and Belgium was nevertheless critical, for on its capacity to attract the best of the French and British mobile forces

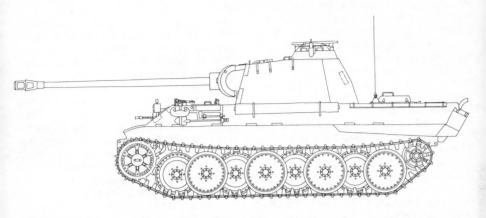

Panzer Mark V (Panther)

Designed as an antidote to the Russian T34, the Panther mounted a long 75 mm gun and had a high cross country speed. *Weight:* 50 tons. *Range:* 60 miles. *Crew:* 5.

northward would depend the success of the Panzer Group's breakthrough in the centre. It had therefore been allotted three of the panzer divisions and a number of Germany's handful of motorized units, including the *Leibstandarte* and *Standarte Der Führer* from the *Verfugungsdivision*. The other two *Standarten* were held in Army Group reserve. *Totenkopf* was in Army High Command (OKH) reserve on the Rhine, and *Polizei* had been assigned for static duty to Army Group C, which was to spend most of the campaign staring balefully at the Maginot Line.

Leibstandarte and *Der Führer*, on the other hand, seized the limelight and the laurels at the opening salvo. *Leibstandarte* had been assigned a leading role in the plan to secure crossing points by *coup de main* into the central Dutch redoubt, formed by canal and river lines around the five major Dutch cities of Amsterdam,

Rotterdam, Utrecht, Leyden, and The Hague. The bridges themselves were to be captured by parachute and air-landed infantry, which were to be relieved by motorised columns deployed before H-hour immediately in front of the Dutch frontier posts. In the event, after a lightning advance to the River IJssel *Leibstandarte* failed to prevent an unusually alert covering force from blowing the essential spans. It was nevertheless able to find an alternative crossing place at Zutphen (where Sir Philip Sydney had died in battle four centuries before), to make another forty-five miles before darkness fell on 10th May. The total distance covered by the regiment in this first day of the campaign was 135 miles, one of the most remarkable contested advances of the war and a frightening warning of what a fully motorised unit could achieve against a purely static enemy.

Der Führer, vanguard of the *Verfu-*

gungsdivision, also secured crossings over the IJssel on 10th May and in the days following, re-united with its parent formation and was hotly engaged in the battle for the Dutch national redoubt. One half of the division found itself committed to an encounter action with the left wing of the First French Army, which had advanced into south Holland, the other, with *Leibstandarte*, continued its drive towards Rotterdam. The French were fairly quickly turfed out of their advanced positions and shortly withdrew from Holland for good, but the Dutch defenders of the Rotterdam water line were less easily overawed. Impatient at the delay, OKH decided to collapse the resistance by terror and on the afternoon of 14th May unleashed a concentrated aerial bombardment on the city. Within a quarter of an hour, its centre had been reduced to smoking ruins and the troops defending its perimeter almost immediately offered their surrender. Among the Germans who raced forward to receive it were troopers of the *Leibstandarte* who, in an excess of excitement, were careless enough with their weapons seriously to wound the commander of the German airborne troops, General Student.

The Waffen SS Units which had fought in Holland now received orders to transfer south into France, where the German breakthrough from the Ardennes was already threatening, as planned, to cut the Allied forces in two. *Totenkopf*, hitherto in OKH reserve, was already on its way. On 19th May it arrived at Cambrai to join forces with 7th Panzer Division. This, Rommel's command, had made breakneck progress since it had crossed the Meuse a week before but, like all the panzer divisions of the spearhead, was now urgently in need of infantry support to clear points of resistance and occupy ground, tasks for which it was constitutionally unsuited. For the next two days *Totenkopf* blooded itself in a series of small mopping-up operations and on

21st May, a day after the leading panzers had reached the Channel near Abbeville, formed up in column of route with 7th Panzer to move on to Arras.

It was just to the south of that town, on the afternoon of 21st May, that Rommel and Eicke, the concentration camp chief who commanded *Totenkopf*, were taught a sharp lesson in the dangers of over-confidence. It had for some days been obvious to the Allied High Command that the long flanks of the German armoured spearhead were vulnerable to counter-attacks and frantic efforts had been made to assemble a suitable force to mount such an operation. Because of its original committment to a strategy of linear defence, uncommitted reserves were now hard to come by but eventually two battalions of the Royal Tank Regiment and an infantry brigade of the British Expeditionary Force were concentrated north of Arras. Soon after 1400, the leading British tanks took Rommel's infantry and armoured regiments in flank and began to knock them about very seriously. Though poorly armed, their tanks' armour was impervious both to German tank and infantry anti-tank guns and it was only when the anti-aircraft gunners of 7th Panzer, deploying their 88mm for the first time in this role, organised a stop-line in open country to the south of Arras that the British thrust was brought to a halt. *Totenkopf* was but lightly engaged in this action but shared something of the shock which afflicted Rommel, who reported that he had been hit by five British armoured divisions. Halted in their tracks, the two divisions were shortly afterwards shifted onto a more northerly axis, OKH and Hitler having decided that the threat to the flanks of the panzer salient must be squashed by a direct assault on the British lines to the south of Dunkirk.

Both *Totenkopf* and *Verfugungs-division*, and the *Leibstandarte* as well, were to be committed to this operation and it was by any reckoning an extremely testing task with which they were faced. For although Dunkirk is now regarded as a 'miracle', a look at the map quickly demonstrates how ideally suited to defence was the outer perimeter which the British had chosen to defend. On the sector which the *Verfugungs* and *Totenkopf* divisions were to attack, two water lines – the La Bassée canal and the upper reaches of the River Lys – interposed serious obstacles, and over neither did the divisions cross without serious casualties. *Standarte Deutschland*, commanded by Felix Steiner, attacking single-handed and unsupported across the Lys, beat off a determined British armoured counterattack from the advanced bridgehead it seized, and lost almost a whole company in doing so. It was saved from worse harm by the unexpected arrival of an anti-tank unit of *Totenkopf*, which had not, as a division, managed to keep up with *Verfugungsdivision's* pace.

This was chiefly due to the devotion with which the infantry of the British 2nd Division had carried out their orders to hold to the last around Béthune. One of the battalions so ordered, the 2nd Royal Norfolks, fought all day in a group of farm and village buildings around a spot called Le Paradis but, having by late afternoon been reduced to less than a company's strength and being almost out of ammunition, decided to surrender. Their white flag was acknowledged by the 2nd *Standarte* of *Totenkopf* and the survivors, ninety-eight in number including many wounded, were marched away. Within a few minutes they had been lined up in a meadow near an adjoining farm and, at the orders of a company commander, Fritz Knochlein, machine-gunned. Any survivors were bayoneted or pistolled.

Two, however, had been overlooked and dragged themselves away that night in a rainstorm to lie up. After being tended by French civilians, they were eventually found by an army unit, taken to hospital and interned. Neither, on repatriation, could at first convince the British army authorities that they were indeed the survivors of a massacre and it was not until 1948 that the author of the crime was at last brought to justice. His crime had aroused considerable ill-feeling in the division at the time and had provoked an official enquiry, but the affair was subsequently hushed up and forgotten, largely because of the refusal by the SS to admit the *Wehrmacht's* competence to investigate it. Sufficient human and documentary evidence was nevertheless assembled by the British Military prosecution to prove the case against Knochlein and he was hanged in Hamburg in October 1948. In the intervening war years, he had won both the Iron Cross and the Knight's Cross and had been promoted Lieutenant-Colonel.

The Le Paradis massacre was a disturbing foretaste of the sort of behaviour unprotected prisoners might expect to receive at the hands, not of every Waffen SS man, but at those of the not uncommon sort which Knochlein typified. For he belonged to that underprivileged class of young Germans whose lives the SS had remade. Forced to leave high school when his father lost his job, he had worked as an errand boy, insurance salesman and clerk, until, in 1934, he was accepted into one of the first *Verfugung* units. He had then been selected for the Brunswick cadet school and after training returned as a platoon commander to *Standarte Deutschland*. In 1940, he had been transferred as a company commander to its depot, which was located in the centre of the Dachau concentration camp complex. Given the number of others who shared this pattern of training it may be thought surprising that Le Paradis is an isolated incident. The campaign, however, was short and the respect for the rules of war still strong on the German side. In the more brutal and less closely super-

France 1940. *Above:* Mortar crew of Standarte *Germania*. *Below:* SS company headquarters group, with British prisoner

vised conditions of fighting in Russia, the Knochleins were to come into their own.

The Waffen SS took but a minor part in the final drive to reduce the Dunkirk perimeter, chiefly because Hitler was now anxious to conserve his mobile units for the second stage of the Battle of France, which he was not convinced would go as easily as the first. In that judgement, he was of course wrong, the battle rapidly developing, once the Somme river-line had been broken through, into a headlong pursuit of the shattered and dismembered French forces which remained. In that pursuit all the Waffen SS formations ran well to the front, the *Leibstandarte* penetrating further south than any other German unit before the announcement of the armistice. At this stage of the fighting even *Polizei*, poor relations of the Waffen SS, managed to join the battle, though at a point where the difficulty of the terrain in the Argonne, and the high

quality of the French defenders who belonged to the Maginot line garrison, denied it any chance to shine.

No glimmer of lustre was shed on the Waffen SS as a whole, however, by the army's reports from the front, which scrupulously forbore to refer to its existence. It had, nevertheless, usually been found where the fighting was thickest and had done as much as its limited size allowed to bring about the German victory. Its achievement was due, of course, partly to the fact that all of its units, apart from *Polizei*, were motorised formations and hence committed always to the wake of the panzers; but due also to the high physical quality of its soldiers and to their remarkable dedication to war. Hitler himself was glad to acknowledge its contribution and distributed decorations to Waffen SS leaders with a liberal hand: more satisfyingly from Himmler's point of view, in August he authorised the establishment of a new Waffen SS division, the fourth to be created since September 1939.

As in the spring, however, the grant of authority alone was not sufficient to conjure the troops into existence. The young conscripts whom OKH allowed to volunteer for the Waffen SS were needed as replacements for the field divisions, and the personnel of the *Totenkopfstandarten* had been earmarked by Himmler for other purposes: to form additional, unauthorised field units and to provide him with an armed police for his private designs. If he were not to dip into this pool of manpower, he must find volunteers from some other source. It was here that ideology suggested a solution. The SS in general, and Himmler in particular, held more closely than most Nazis to the 'Nordic' ideal – that of the blond super-race – and through the Wehrmacht's conquests of Denmark, Norway, Holland and Belgium, much of its homeland had been brought under German rule. It had also been brought, like the settlement areas of the *Volksdeutsche* of Poland and Czechoslovakia, within range of the SS recruiting agencies, and yet remained outside the writ of the Reich recruiting laws. In theory, therefore, many thousands of racially acceptable youths had become available as recruits, if they could be persuaded to volunteer.

As the Germans had quickly discovered, there was in fact a fairly widespread disposition to do so in the conquered lands, where Nazi-style parties – in Norway, Quisling's *Nasjonal Samling*, in Holland, Mussert's *Nationaal-Socialistiche Beweging*, in Belgium, Degrelle's *Rexists*, had all attracted sizeable membership before the war. Among their youth sections, Gottlob Berger's commissars had

An MG-34 crew of Standarte
Deutschland behind a dyke in
Holland, May 1940

already found sufficient volunteers to
recruit two regiments, *Nordland*, composed of Danes and Norwegians,
Westland, composed of Dutchmen and
Flemish-speaking Belgians. By
December, they had been brought,
under the supervision of German
officers and NCOs, to a high enough

state of training to be embodied into
the new division, for which Himmler
chose the romantic title of *Wiking*.
(Viking). Its third regiment was found
by the transfer from the *Verfugungsdivision* of *Standarte Germania*. Felix
Steiner, former colonel of *Deutschland*
and the winner of a Knight's Cross in
France, was appointed general
commanding.

Himmler undertook at the same
time a re-organisation of his Waffen

SS units as a whole, designed as always to increase the number available for service in the field. *Verfugungsdivision* was given another of the *Totenkopfstandarten* in exchange for *Germania* and was re-titled *Das Reich*. Another two *Totenkopfstandarten* were brigaded as *Kampfgruppe Nord* (later to become a division) and a third, re-titled SS Infantry Regiment 9, was put under army control and posted to Northern Norway on garri-

son duty. This left another five *Totenkopfstandarten* and two SS cavalry regiments still at Himmler's disposal, out of which he formed two SS brigades, armed for field duty but remaining under his personal direction.

The order of battle of the Waffen SS by the spring of 1941, stood therefore at four divisions (*Das Reich, Totenkopf, Polizei* and *Wiking*), two brigades (*Leibstandarte Adolf Hitler* and *Nord*)

SS light machine-gunner, Holland 1940

and one infantry regiment, albeit that these figures had only been achieved by very hurried measures. Himmler's anxiety to expand his field force is understandable in the light of his knowledge of Hitler's plans for the invasion of Russia. The preliminary order for *Barbarossa* (Führer Directive No 21) had been issued in December 1940 and Himmler had recognised from the first that the coming campaign offered his soldiers, of whose ideological purity he made even more in his talks with Hitler than of their military efficiency, the chance to prove their peculiar usefulness in a struggle between opposed political systems and superior and inferior races. It was very much part of his argument, in his appeals to Hitler for a bigger share of young German manhood, that the Waffen SS and its leaders, unlike the Wehrmacht and its generals, were psychologically attuned to a war in which no quarter would be shown.

In the spring of 1941, therefore, the motorised Waffen SS was drafted eastward, along with the bulk of the German field army, to take up stations on the frontiers of Russia. Before all could take their places, however, an outbreak of anti-Nazi activity in the Balkans, coupled with a series of humiliating setbacks inflicted by the Greek army on the Italians who had unwisely attacked it, imposed a displacement of force southward, and a consequent postponement of the planned launch of Barbarossa. The ensuing campaign made little demand on the expertise of the Waffen SS, and caused it few casualties, but it provided the greener units with valuable experience of the realities of combat. For Hitler, though the campaign had lasted only three weeks, it caused a grave, perhaps a decisive, postponement of the attack date he had set for Barbarossa. Scheduled originally for 15th May, it was not now to be unleashed until 22nd June 1941.

71

Crusade in the east

It has become fashionable to question whether Hitler's decision to attack Russia was the outcome of any long-laid plan, a number of historians being ready to argue that Hitler's talk of *Lebensraum* and of Germany's destiny to lord it over the inferior races of the Slav lands was purely emotive in purpose. In their view Hitler's decision was dictated by short-term calculations, and the fact that he had spoken, often and for many years, of the 'coming struggle with Bolshevism' attests to nothing but his well known relish for blood-curdling rhetoric.

That may well be. But whatever inner reservations Hitler may have made, the effect of his speeches and writings on his captive audience of Germans, many of whom undoubtedly wished to hear exactly that sort of message, was bound to be inflammatory. Nor was it only the little man over whom Hitler cast his anti-Bolshevik spell. Many of the grandees of the movement were committed to the idea of *Lebensraum;* some like Rosenburg, had built their careers on it, and others like Himmler, asked nothing better than the opportunity to put the idea into action.

Anti-Bolshevism and the doctrine of racial superiority had been from the first an integral part of the training of all SS men, and those who had been selected for the cadet academies had received particularly strong doses. No one preached the message better than Himmler himself. The flavour of his thoughts on the subject is perfectly conveyed in a speech he made to reinforcements for *Kampfgruppe Nord* in the first month of the Barbarossa Campaign.

'To you SS men I need not say much. For years – over a decade – we old National Socialists have struggled in Germany with Bolshevism, with Communism. One thing we can be certain of today: what we predicted in our political battle was not exaggerated by one single word and sentence. On the contrary, it was too mild and too weak because we did not, at that time, yet have the insight we have today. It is a great heavenly blessing that, for the first time in a thousand years, fate has given us this Führer. It is a stroke of fate that the Führer, in his turn, decided, at the right moment, to upset Russia's plans, and thus prevent a Russian attack. This is an ideological battle and a struggle of races. Here in this struggle stands National Socialism: an ideology based on the value of our Germanic, Nordic blood. Here stands a word as we have conceived it: beautiful, decent, socially equal, that perhaps, in a few instances is still burdened by shortcomings, but as a whole, a happy, beautiful world full of culture; this is what our Germany is like. On the other side stands a population of 180 million, a mixture of races, whose very names are unpronounceable, and whose physique is such that one can shoot them down without pity or compassion. These animals, that torture and ill-treat every prisoner from our side, every wounded man that they come across and do not treat them the way decent soldiers would, you will see for yourself. These people have been welded by the Jews into one religion, one ideology, that is called Bolshevism, with the task: now we have Russia, half of Asia, a part of Europe, now we will overwhelm Germany and the whole world.

'When you, my men, fight over there in the East, you are carrying on the same struggle, against the same sub-humanity, the same inferior races, that at one time appeared under the name of Huns, another time – 1,000 years ago at the time of King Henry and Otto I – under the name of Magyars, another time under the name of Tartars, and still another time under the name of Genghis Khan and the Mongols. Today they appear as Russians under the political banners of Bolshevism.'

The misery of victory. SS troops in Russia, 1941

Needless to say, Himmler's historical views were as crackpot as those of his on diet, medicine or biology. But while judgements on the nutritive value of raw oatmeal, however eccentric, can do little harm even to those who hold them, historical misrepresentation, if trumpeted strongly and consistently enough by men of power, can kill. And there is little doubt that many victims of the Russian war, not of the extermination operations but of the fighting and its aftermath, owed their deaths to the indoctrination which their enemies, among whom the Waffen SS were soon to show themselves foremost, had received before and continued to receive throughout the war. For Himmler and his agents very successfully convinced large numbers, perhaps a majority of the Waffen SS, that their opponents were indeed sub-human, that the killing of however many of them consequently counted for very little, and that since their leaders willed nothing less than the extinction of Germany and her people, the struggle must take the form of one of annihilation.

In the vast rear-areas of the eastern front, which fell so quickly to the German onset and were transferred as quickly to Himmler's authority (as German police leader), the work of annihilation, chiefly of Jews but also of any elements held hostile to Germany, was undertaken swiftly, methodically and without pity. At the front, on the other hand, the conduct of the fighting soldiers, their energies in any case engaged to the full with the fulfilment of day-to-day military tasks, was comparatively unmarred by atrocity – or so it has ever after been claimed. (Many thousands of executed prisoners would cry from the grave that that was not always so). But between the operational front and the 'settled' zone on the borders of the Reich, stretched an enormous belt of territory, partly under direct military government, partly under that of the Reichskommissars, in which Himmler was to prosecute a running campaign against the partisans who immediately sprang to life there. In the process many thousands of innocents were to die, either by way of reprisals or as 'suspects' rounded up in sweeps through the countryside: 15,000 'partisans' for example, killed in a drive round Lake Pelik in August 1943, yielded only 1,100 rifles as booty. That group fell, as it happened, to the guns of the enlisted criminals of Dirlewanger's brigade, a crew of whom even the least fastidious fought shy. Many victims, however, were shot down in cold blood by the men of front-line units temporarily detached for anti-partisan warfare, or detailed for extermination duty while on rest.

The ferocity with which some at least of the Waffen SS were prepared to act in the rear areas of the Russian front had been indicated from the first by their ruthless performance in battle – and in this respect the reputation of Himmler's divisions was of course already high before 22nd June 1941 but at that time their fame was not widespread; by the end of the year no soldier of the German army could fail to have been aware of it.

This sudden publicisation the Waffen SS owed to several factors: to the fact that almost all its divisions were motorised, and therefore fought always with the leading units; to its remarkable fighting qualities; and to the distribution of its units between all three of Hitler's Army Groups, so that it made a contribution to operations across the whole front.

Hitler's plan for the invasion envisaged an advance in three divergent directions: towards Leningrad in the north by Army Group C: towards Moscow in the centre by Army Group B; and towards Kiev and the Ukraine in the south by Army Group A. These were territorial objectives. But he also demanded – and anticipated – the destruction of the Red Army en route. The Wehrmacht had therefore not merely to make ground but also to encircle and destroy the Russian

Above : SS anti-aircraft gunners scan Soviet skies, 1941. *Below left :* SS anti-tank gunners engage Russian armour on the edge of a wood, August 1941. *Below right :* On Napoleon's route to Moscow, August 1941

formation which barred their path. The tactics of the invasion demanded the concentration of the panzer and motorised divisions into compact groups which were to advance at the fastest speed possible, leaving centres of resistance and unengaged enemy formations to be overcome by the slower-moving infantry columns.

Since the Germans deployed only nineteen panzer and twelve motorised divisions, the five Waffen SS divisions were to perform a role out of all proportion to their numbers. *Leibstandarte* and *Wiking* were attached to Army Group A; *Das Reich* to Army Group B; *Totenkopf* and *Polizei* to Army Group C. The last were to play comparatively the least striking part in the summer and autumn battles, beginning as reserve formations and spending some months in the later stages encircled in the Demiansk pocket near Leningrad. *Das Reich*, committed in the centre where the decisive thrust was to be made with the bulk of the armour (ten out of nineteen divisions) achieved on the other hand a notable record of success. It took part in the great encirclement battle of Smolensk in August, then in the battle for Kiev on the southern front and was finally transferred to the Moscow front for the winter battle before the city, having been part of Guderian's panzer group throughout. *Leibstandarte* and *Wiking* were deployed from the outset on the Kiev axis. The former was in the spearhead which reached the Black Sea coast in August and by November, it had reached to as far as Rostov on the Don.

Dramatic though the events of these five months of fighting were, the outcome did not yield the results which Hitler had hoped for. To what extent this was due to his own indecision and miscalculation remains a matter of dispute, but since it was he who exerted the major influence over German strategy, the responsibility must be judged as chiefly his. The principal area of controversy is over his decision to switch the bulk of the armour from the central to the southern army group in August, (the decision which entailed *Das Reich's* transfer to the Kiev battle) and his subsequent but belated appreciation of the importance of Moscow, leading to a redeployment of armour to the centre again. The generals, in particular the panzer general Guderian, argued with him in vain that a threat to Moscow, the communication centre of western Russia, would force the Russians to fight a battle of decision there, where a German victory, of which he was certain, would give them possession of the whole of White Russia and the Ukraine. Hitler declared himself unconvinced, however, that a battle for Moscow could be guaranteed to yield those results, and ordered that the territories he coveted be seized by direct assault. By the time his armies were on the way to doing so, and the armour had been redeployed, the campaigning season was drawing to its close. The Battle of Moscow, into whose suburbs patrols of Army Group B penetrated on 4th December, was therefore fought in the snow.

It was not, moreover, fought on the Wehrmacht's terms. Overstretched and unequipped for winter warfare, the German armoured and infantry divisions broke on the fixed defences of Moscow, while the counter-surge of a Russian offensive, mounted by hardened Siberian divisions of the Far Eastern Army, washed over their flanks. And not only on the Moscow front did the Rusians show that, despite all their lost millions they still retained the power to attack, in late November they recaptured Rostov (in an action which decimated the *Leibstandarte*) and seemed ready to win back ground on a major scale in the Ukraine. These widespread reverses threw the high command of the German army into panic. Faced apparently by armies of automatons, sprung fully-armed from the frozen steppe, Hitler's generals urged retreat with a single voice, retreat to a shorter

Above: Latvian volunteers of the Waffen SS are decorated with the Iron Cross (Second Class). Below: An SS reconnaissance team re-groups after a river crossing

line, above all retreat to a zone where houses still stood, in which their frozen soldiers could wait out the winter.

Hitler, whose knowledge of history was patchy but in some spots sound, would have none of it. Retreat, he rightly insisted, would certainly complete the destruction of the Wehrmacht; it must hold where it stood. Units that were overrun would be written off: the gaps could be plugged from the reserves, and in the winter campaign that this Führer decree brought about, many units were lost without trace. But the majority held and none more tenaciously than those of the Waffen SS. By the coming of spring, their superiority was firmly established in the Führer's mind and so too were the inklings of a new plan for their employment.

'Reinforce success' is as good an organisational as a tactical principle, and the plan Hitler had in mind for Himmler's divisions amounted just to that. He would, he decided, withdraw them when and as they could be spared, transfer them to a quiet theatre and fit them out as 'panzer-grenadiers'. This was a new German army concept, or rather the amplification of one already well-tested. It had long been recognised that mobile infantry was an essential complement to the panzer divisions, but it had also become increasingly evident that lorried formations lacked the punch and cross-country performance to keep up close enough with the tanks. The decision was therefore taken to equip all motorised divisions with tracked and half-tracked personnel carriers and to supply them, where possible, with a battalion of tanks or tank destroyers. The resulting augmentation of power both in attack and defence proved remarkable, and Hitler was sure that the effect would be even more heightened when equipment of that sort was put in the hands of his élite.

During the summer and autumn of 1942, therefore, *Leibstandarte*, *Das*

Reich, and *Totenkopf* were, one by one, withdrawn to France. In fact, each had already received its tank battalion, as had *Wiking*, though the latter was compelled to adapt itself to its new role actually in the field. And that role was a particularly demanding one for *Wiking*, for as part of Kleist's panzer group, it was to fight its way with the southern army group – miraculously revivified after the winter ordeal – into the oil-rich isthmus of the Caucasus between the Black and Caspian Seas. That exploit, in which *Wiking* was throughout in the forefront, was linked of course with the great advance of late summer of 1942 to the Volga at Stalingrad, and

An SS man disregards local
intelligence, Russia, 1941

ts outcome was irretrievably bound
.p with the ebb and flow of the fighting
or that city.

Stalingrad was not, fortunately for
he reputation of the Waffen SS
ivisions, to be their battle. By the
ime it was fully joined only three SS
ivisions, *Wiking, Polizei* and *Nord* – the
atter engaged on the Finnish front as
art of the Twentieth Mountain Army
remained in the east. The recovery
rom Stalingrad, on the other hand,
as to involve the refurbished *Leib-
andarte, Totenkopf* and *Das Reich* in
hat perhaps was their most notable
peration.

The double envelopment of Stalin-
rad, which brought about the

entombment of the Sixth Army in
November, had carried the Russian
front by February 1943 to beyond the
Donets, over two hundred miles west
of the line held by the Germans at the
floodtide of their 1942 offensive. The
Russian offensive had by now run out
of steam, but no one on the German
side was foolish enough to think that
the enemy would not resume the
attack as soon as they could. How
best to counter this offensive had
become therefore the most pressing
command decision of the moment.

It was one Hitler would not face up

Above: SS cavalrymen in their second Russian winter, February 1943. *Above right:* An SS section commander rests after the breakout from Charkov, March 1943. *Below right:* An officer and NCO of the Leibstandarte at a pre-attack briefing, Russia, September, 1941

to, for though he had exercised the function of Army Commander-in-Chief since early 1942, his confidence in his powers of judgement had been badly shaken by the results of Stalingrad. Effective leadership therefore devolved upon General von Manstein, commanding Army Group South on the critical front, and his solution, determined by his belief that the numerically inferior Germans could only wage war on equal terms with the Russians by exploiting their superiority in mobile operations, was to abandon the principle of 'unyielding defence' and set about organising an armoured counter-attack, designed to converge on the Russian salient at Kharkov from three separate directions. To do so he asked for, and was given, twelve panzer divisions – the

most powerful force of tanks yet assembled in war.

Three of these, the three 'classic' SS divisions as they have been called, *Leibstandarte*, *Totenkopf* and *Das Reich*, formed one of the two arms of the pincer with which Manstein planned to bite out the Russian salient around Kharkov, into which the impetus of their onrush from Stalingrad had carried them. *Leibstandarte* and *Das Reich* had been badly cut up in the defences of Kharkov in February, and *Totenkopf* had lost its commander – the unlovable Eicke of the first concentration camp – the day after it had arrived in a reinforcement role from France on 28th February. Nevertheless, the three – now formed into the first SS Corps under Hausser, the original commander of *Verfugungs-*

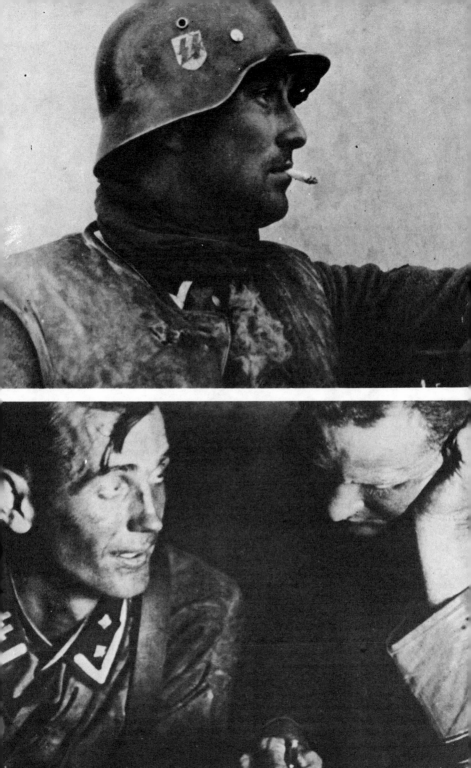

Above: SS field security police flush
Russians out of a barn at gunpoint,
1941
Right: Summary execution; the SS man
in the centre has just shot one of the
captives in the back

division – were a formidable team,
equipped as they were with rather
more tanks than the average army
panzer division, including companies
of the new Tigers. Striking south-east
on 23rd February, they concluded five
days' hard fighting by making a junc-
tion with the Fourth Panzer Army on
28th February, then, turning north,
the combined force drove to the
investment of Kharkov which, after a
desperate defence, the Russians abandoned on 14th March. In doing so, the
Russians surrendered a belt of territory over fifty miles deep and left on
the battlefield 600 tanks and over
20,000 dead. But in the same period,
Hausser's SS Panzer Corps suffered
nearly 12,000 casualties.

It had nevertheless emerged as a
task force of lethal capability, and
was therefore typecast for the next
round of operations which the Army
General Staff had to contemplate in

the spring of 1943. Were those operations to be offensive or defensive?
Many factors argued for the defensive.

Germany was weakening as a military power, of that there could be no
doubt. North Africa was lost, the
Balkans had become a running sore,
the air attack on the homeland was
gathering force. The Russian armies
were stronger than they had ever been
before and better equipped, while the
German divisions were undergoing a
net decline in numbers and weapon-
strength, so that from four battalions
of tanks with an establishment of
eighty each in 1942, panzer divisions
had been reduced by mid-1943 to two

battalions of about fifty each, with a third battalion of tank-destroyers. The machines themselves had certainly improved in quality, the tincan Mark I and IIs having been replaced by Mark III and IVs, while the Tiger (though in limited numbers) and the first of the Panthers was beginning to appear from the factories. Nevertheless too much was being asked of too little and there were the strongest arguments, advanced vehemently by numbers of senior German generals, for husbanding the armour as a mobile reserve force and fighting meanwhile a strictly defensive war in the east.

Zeitzler, however, now Chief of the Army General Staff, would not hear such arguments. Rather, he argued, Germany's progressive decline could only be halted by shock action, designed to knock the Red Armies off balance before their recovery made further headway. The spot he chose for this assault was the Kursk salient, overhanging the Kharkov battlefield, whose flanks invited the kind of pincer attack which had yielded such enor-

mous hauls of prisoners in the summer battles of 1941. Manstein was sceptical, Guderian openly hostile; Hitler hesitated, his confidence still not recovered since the Stalingrad debacle. He was determined, in any case, to risk nothing until sufficient Tigers and Panthers to refit the armoured reserve were available.

By July after several postponements, he felt assured enough to give his consent to the plan. It entailed the concentration of two 'panzer wedges' against the Kursk salient, one to drive south, the other north, until the two met. By far the more powerful was the southern group, which deployed nine divisions along a front of less than thirty miles. Six were army divisions, the other three the 'classics' of the SS Panzer Corps. All were to adopt the same tactics, in which the tip of the armoured wedge was formed by the heaviest tanks, in this case Tigers, and the edges of the arrowhead by the lighter Mark IV s and Panthers. Infantry, as was now commonplace, was thin on the ground, most of the

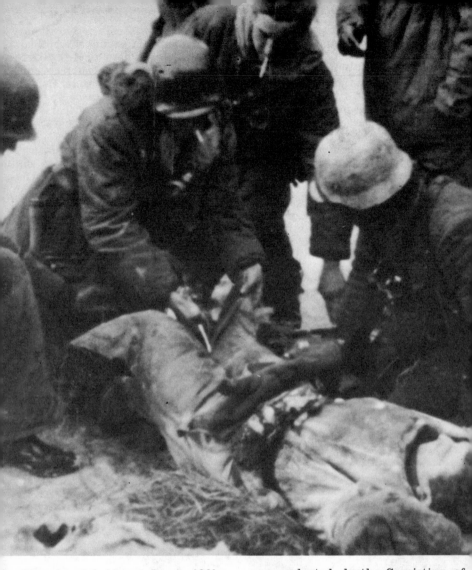

SS regimental aid post, Russia, 1941

ordinary foot divisions being tied to a static role and the panzer-grenadiers, as the infantry of the mobile divisions was now called, being consequently overworked.

It is doubtful whether a better balanced force would have made much difference to the outcome. Operation Citadel was a battle foredoomed, as even Hitler had scented, for the Russian position was organised in unprecedented depth. Consisting of three main zones, each of up to five lines of trenches and with subsidiary positions to the rear, its approaches were scattered with mines at a density of 5,000 to the square mile and covered by the fire of 20,000 pieces of artillery. Six thousand of these were 76mm anti-tank guns, arranged in batteries under unified control, and supported by well-concealed groups of tank-hunting infantrymen. The position, in short, was as near impregnable as

of the attack the battle began to go wrong for the Germans on the northern flank. Model's panzer divisions, equipped with a model of Tiger which mounted no machine gun, quickly lost their lighter tanks on the Russian perimeter, only to see their heavies hunted down by Russian tank-killing squads. Manstein's Tigers on the southern flank also became separated from their accompanying units but were at least able to defend themselves until the infantry fought their way up. On the succeeding days, however, the brunt of the fighting fell increasingly on the dwindling tank formations, which were only with the greatest difficulty able to deepen the pockets they had opened. The SS Corps found itself in particularly desperate straits, its three divisions being unable to make contact across the separate breaches they had made.

On 12th July, having advanced only nine miles at a cost of 1,400 tanks knocked out, Hoth, the Fourth Panzer Army commander, determined on one last fling into the gap. Assembling the remaining 600 tanks of the two army and the SS Corps, he ordered them to break out, regardless of the danger to their flanks, into open country. By midday, they were locked in combat with a fresh Russian army. Eight hours later they were beaten. New Soviet equipment of unheralded power, and above all an enormous Soviet superiority in numbers, had driven them from the field. Next day, Hitler shut the battle down.

This 'death ride of the panzers', if it had not lost Hitler an already hopeless war, had effectively deprived him of any freedom of action in the future. The 1,000 odd tanks irrevocably thrown away had constituted his last grand strategic reserve. Without it, he would henceforth have to fight when and where the enemy dictated, no longer having the means to take initiatives of his own.

This was not to say that he would no longer need an armoured striking force; indeed he would need one more

any that has ever been attacked.

On 5th July 1943, the panzers drove against it, hopefully inspired by a Führer order of the day. 'Soldiers of the Reich', it read, 'this day you are to take part in an offensive of such importance that the whole future of the war may depend upon its outcome. More than anything else, your victory will show the whole world that resistance to the power of the German Army is hopeless'. Vain encouragement; almost from the first moments

Above : SS reconnaissance team on snowshoes, February, 1942. *Right :* SS sub-machine gunner marches on the point, Russia. *Below :* SS Panzer-grenadiers form up for an attack on the Toropez front, January 1943

than ever, in order to plug the gaps which would undoubtedly appear in his overstretched lines and to mount local counter-attacks. It was in this sort of operation, which demanded an ability to keep cool and show grit when the front was collapsing, that the Waffen SS divisions had already particularly distinguished themselves, and it was therefore entirely logical that Hitler should decide in consequence to add to their numbe on a major scale during 1943. I December 1942 he had authorised th recruitment of two new panzer grenadier divisions, 9th *Hohenstauffe* (named after the family of the firs German Emperors) and 10th *Frunds berg* (named after the founder of th 16th Century *Landsknechte*, thos German freebooters of whom Himmle liked to think the Waffen SS were th

the same time, the best of the Waffen SS divisions were remustered as panzer divisions: 1st *Leibstandarte*, 2nd *Das Reich*, 3rd *Totenkopf*, 5th *Wiking* and the new 9th, 10th and 12th. These seven divisions amounted to almost a quarter of Germany's panzer strength (thirty divisions), a proportion which was to be maintained and even to grow as the war drew out.

The increase in the establishment of the Waffen SS was matched by no balancing inflow of volunteers to fill out the new formations. Himmler, however, had now very much strengthened his position in dealing with the army over enlistments and, for the raising of *Hohenstauffen* and *Frundsberg*, simply drafted the numbers he needed from the pool of recruits, in all between seventy and eighty per cent of the divisional complements. Increasingly, and despite his proclaimed insistence on the voluntary principle, he was to be forced to do the same in the future, both to raise new units and provide replacements for the old. None of his subsequent creations, however, were to be German in the sense that the original *Leibstandarte* had been; and none were ever again to measure up, of course, to the physical excellence of its material.

Indeed, already well before the expansion programme of 1943, Himmler had been compelled to authorise the acceptance of large numbers of non-Germans into the Waffen SS, enthusiastically in the case of the 'Germanics' of Scandinavia and the Low Countries, but only with much self-justification in the case of the unarguably non-Nordic races. It was, however, upon these two sources of recruitment that he was principally to draw in building up his numbers from 1943 onwards, with the result that the Waffen SS, conceived as a German volunteer élite, was progressively to be transformed into a non-Nordic, conscript mass.

spiritual heirs). In June, Hitler had accepted Reich Youth Leader Axmann's offer to raise a division from the Hitler Youth, which became 12th *Hitler Jugend*; the average age of the volunteers was seventeen. And in October, he ordered the raising of two new panzer-grenadier divisions, 16th *Reichsführer SS* and 17th *Götz von Berlichingen* (named after a German robber-baron of the middle ages). At

The foreign legions

Himmler's enthusiasm for a foreign SS was of long standing. But it was also in origin an enthusiasm of a strictly partial sort and strongly romantic in flavour. The foreign volunteers whom he wished to enlist were to be pure Nordic types and the cause he wished them to espouse was not that of their fatherlands but of his own muddled and dangerous idealism of 'race, blood and soil'. 'We must attract all the Nordic blood in the world to us,' he told the officers of the *Leibstandarte* in September 1940, 'depriving our enemies of it, so that never again will Nordic or Germanic blood fight against us.' Later he was to speak of incorporating the 'millions of Germans living in America'. He had in fact authorised the recruitment of foreign volunteers as early as 1938 and the hundred who had been accepted by 1940 included five Americans. The majority, however, were German Swiss, though neither of these nationalities came forward in any numbers once the war had begun.

It was at that point, of course, that Himmler's permissive attitude towards foreign recruitment was transformed into an active enthusiasm. The army's niggardly release of native German volunteers from the manpower pool compelled the SS to look elsewhere for recruits for the new field divisions and the *Volksdeutsche* of Germany's eastern neighbours provided the most obvious source. The Balkan campaign of 1941 opened up a new reservoir, for Rumania, Hungary and Yugoslavia sheltered large communities of racial Germans, to whose young men enlistment in the SS seemed to offer the most immediate outlet for a great deal of pent-up resentment at their minority status. Far from being promoted to positions of authority over their Slav fellow-citizens, however, these early *Volksdeutsche* recruits to the Waffen SS found themselves embodied as private

Danish volunteer battalion marches into Germany, 1941

soldiers, in ordinary field formations, shortly destined to be committed to operations against Russia.

Since the *Volksdeutsche* could scarcely lay claim to the status of Germans while disclaiming any obligation to the fatherland, there was little that they could do to object, nor indeed in 1940-41 did many wish to, though later in the war their readiness to volunteer noticeably diminished. It was different, however, with the other 'racially acceptable' group of potential foreign volunteers, the 'Germanics' of Scandinavia and the Low Countries. Himmler recognised from the first that they would have to be promised units of their own if they were to be persuaded to enlist, partly because of the difficulties of language but also because some respect for their independent national status would have to be shown them. Hence the formation of the first two foreign *Standarten*, *Westland* and *Nordland*, raised respectively from Dutchmen and Belgian Flemings and from Danes and Norwegians in June and April 1940. Even so, recruits were so slow in coming forward that the cadres had to be filled out with Germans, and when it was decided to form a division around these two *Standarten*, the third was supplied by transferring *Germania* complete from the *Das Reich* Division. At the outbreak of war with Russia, less than a third of the *Wiking* Division was made up of 'Germanics'.

This was not surprising, for even accepting that there were existing Nazi style parties in several of the conquered European countries whose followers were disposed to sympathise with the Nazi message of a common racial struggle, and also that in all were to be found a proportion of feckless youth who will 'go for a soldier' under any flag, the taboo against taking service in the enemy's ranks is very strong in nation-states. Its breach carries the taint of treachery and cuts the individual off, sometimes irrevocably, from family and friends.

Danish volunteer battalion marches into Germany, 1941

Above left : **Haupsturmführer Per Sörensen, Commander of 1st Company, Danish Volunteer Battalion.** *Above right :* **Cossack machine-gunner of the volunteer units which later became part of the Waffen SS.** *Right :* **Indians in the uniform of the Indian Legion**

Those Germans most closely involved in the matter, principally SS officials, quickly came to recognise that the most promising method of tapping 'Germanic' manpower lay in the offer to raise independent national legions under their own officers. Occupation had deprived many professional soldiers of their career and while the bonds of patriotism were too strong in most cases to allow them to collaborate, a few were sufficiently pro-Nazi in sympathy to provide a nucleus around which such legions could be built; above all, they would be the most likely to win over recruits. A prototype legion was formed in May 1941 from a group of Finns, anxious to revenge themselves on Russia for the dictated peace of 1940, and their toughness and expertise augured well for the formation of others. Very

shortly after the opening of Operation Barbarossa, Hitler gave his assent to the project.

Himmler was at first unwilling, however, to accept any but units of 'kindred stock' into the SS and thus, although he agreed that Scandinavian and Low Country recruits to the Legions need only meet Wehrmacht, not Waffen SS, standards of physical fitness, he would not extend SS status to Frenchmen or Spaniards. It was accordingly arranged that the French Legions should be raised, trained and led by the army and that the SS should have responsibility only for the Dutch, Danish, Norwegian, Belgian Fleming, and Swedish Legions. The latter, after one of its officers had been badly handled by his German superiors, quickly dissolved but the other four, entitled

Freiwilligen Legion Niederlande, Danemark, Norwegen and *Flandern* were all set up in July 1941. The personnel from the Dutch and Belgian Legions was found in part from an experimental mixed Dutch-Belgian *Freiwilligenstandarte Nordwest*, which had been raised under the auspices of the two countries' Nazi-style parties in April 1941; that for the Danish from demobilised soldiers of the Danish army and the Norwegians from a similar source. Some trickery and a little coercion was brought to bear, however, and even so the strength of the Legions hovered well below the minimum necessary for combat efficiency. Officers were difficult to find and, when found, often very understandably resented the hauteur with which they were treated by their German superiors. Those units which lacked officers of their own nationality, notably *Flandern*, also objected strongly to the brutal treatment meted out by their German training staffs. The Legions therefore made slow progress in completing their preparation for action. By the beginning of 1942, only two, the Dutch and Belgian, had entered the line, both on the static Leningrad front. Their numbers amounted to 2,500 and 900. *Norwegen* and *Danemark* each comprised between eleven and twelve hundred men but were both beset by internal troubles. The Danes, in particular, were bitterly divided into pro- and anti-Nazi groups, to which latter both the commanding officer and the second-in-command belonged. It was not until a change of leadership in February that the unit settled down sufficiently to be sent to the eastern front, where it was attached to *Totenkopf*. Shortly before this the Norwegians had been eased into the line near Leningrad.

All four legions spent 1942 in action against the Red Army. By the end of the year, however, the SS leadership was forced to adjudge this experiment in the Nordic alliance a failure. The Finnish battalion, oldest of the volunteer units, had alone performed well, as it was to do until withdrawn for the defence of the homeland in 1943, but then the Finns alone had any real motive for involvement. The Russians were for them ancient oppressors and recent aggressors. The West Europeans had no such reasons for enlisting in the Waffen SS, and its message of anti-Bolshevism and racial brotherhood, allied to an appeal to their spirit of adventure, was inadequate to call forward recruits in any useful number.

In March 1943, it was therefore decided to bring together all West European units of the army and Waffen SS, in order to rationalise the manpower supply. The Danish, Norwegian and Dutch Legions were grouped together to form the *Nordland* Panzer Grenadier Division, its ranks being filled out with large numbers of native Germans. *Flandern*, the Belgian Fleming unit, was broken up, though many of its men eventually found their way to a new formation, the *Sturmbrigade Langemarck*, which was to be raised to the status, though never to reach the strength, of a division towards the end of the war.

At the same time the foreign units of the German army were brought under the aegis of the SS. The most important of these politically was the *Legion Volontaire Francaise*, originally raised by French Fascists as the French Anti-Bolshevik Legion in July 1941, and later sponsored, rather halfheartedly, by the Vichy government as its equivalent to the Spanish Blue Division. This French Legion and the Wallonian Legion, raised by Degrelle's Rexists in French-speaking Belgium, became SS *Freiwilligen Standarten* and eventually, like *Langemarck*, titular divisions, as 28th *Wallonien* and 33rd *Charlemagne*. But it is doubtful if any of these units ever much exceeded the strength of a regiment, say 3,000 men.

Officers of the Yugoslav Muslim mountain division. They are wearing climbing boots as well as the fez

Left: A volunteer for the Danish Legion is interviewed in Copenhagen, 1941.
Above: Flemish volunteers take the oath of loyalty to the Führer, June 1942

In the case of the two Italian divisions which appear in SS records, 24th and 29th, it is even doubtful whether they achieved the status of combat troops, being probably confined to anti-partisan operations in the rump of Mussolini's Italy.

Besides the first-line SS units of West European composition, of which *Wiking* was always the most prestigious, there were also raised a number of second-grade or garrison units, like the *Landstorm-Nederland* division, whose role seems to have been that of a domestic Dutch Nazi Militia. A number of independent regiments of Dutchman was also formed, under German officers, and sent to the Russian front, Holland producing by some way the largest quota of volunteers for the movement, some 50,000 in all during the five years of war. Belgium produced 40,000, Fleming and Walloon in equal proportion, France 20,000 and Denmark and Norway each 6,000. The majority of these came in towards the end of the war, an anachronism best explained in terms of the fears of retribution many young collaborators must have come to feel as the onset of defeat drew nearer. All, of course, were committed to the Russian front and very large numbers died in action, some eventually fell fighting in defence of the ruins of the Reich Chancellery in May, 1945.

Their number did not of course include the volunteers of the British Free Corps, the smallest of the independent foreign contingents, so small indeed that its existence has sometimes been doubted. Exist it certainly did, its members wearing the Union Jack as a sleeve insignia, but they did not exceed fifty or so, all of them renegade prisoners-of-war. For Himmler their importance was purely of a propaganda nature. Much the same can be said of the Indian Legion, also raised from prisoners-of-war captured in the Western Desert, and organised by the extraordinary Subhas Chandra Bose, Gandhi's right wing rival for the leadership of the Indian Independence movement. It eventually reached a strength of 2,000, but was never committed to action. Given the fate of its far more credible brother-organisation, the Indian National Army, which Bose raised for the Japanese from prisoners taken in South-East Asia, that was perhaps as well. Hitler himself had no illusions about the *Legion Indien*, which he described as 'a joke'. In describing the Indians as fit only 'to turn prayer wheels' however, he was merely giving way to his racial prejudices. The plight of the Indians was tragic. Excellent soldiers – when led by Indian officers, or by Britons who knew their villages and spoke their language – they were quite disoriented by capture. Having succumbed to the wiles of Himmler's recruiting agents, they found themselves in the hands of strange and unsympathetic officers and were further afflicted by guilt at having broken their oath of loyalty, to which they attached particular importance. Wisely the British government forbore, when the war was over, to press charges against any but the most flagrant of the ringleaders.

Equally tragic on a much larger scale, was the plight of the *Volksdeutsche* whom Himmler began to enlist, later to conscript, in numbers from 1942 onwards. Their status has already been outlined. In former times treated as privileged settlers by one or other of the four great empires – Russian, Austrian, Prussian, or Turkish – which had divided eastern Europe between them, they found themselves after 1918 reduced to the status of isolated minorities. None could complain objectively of harsh treatment at the hands of the new governments, and the smaller and more scattered communities whose

sense of identity with Germany was weakest, would no doubt in time have successfully assimilated. The rise of Hitler prevented that. His promise of a 'Greater Reich' kept alive the racial Germans' sense of kinship, fed the Slav states' fears and rekindled the mistrust and dislike of their native majorities for the alien minorities. Many of these minorities were sizeable, moreover. In the rump of Czecho-Slovakia lived 250,000 Germans: in Hungary, 500,000: in Rumania, 800,000: in Yugoslavia, Albania and Bulgaria 750,000: in the Baltic States and Russia proper, 250,000; in all, some 2,500,000 foreign nationals, 'German in race and culture' as his experts called them, had been brought by mid-1942 under direct German administration. And of these, large numbers were senselessly uprooted from their homes to be resettled in areas, selected by Himmler's experts, to fit in with his plans for the future political geography of Europe. In the process, many were themselves to become displaced persons, as bitter and frustrated as any to be found wandering the roads of the east or rotting in its camps in those years, but with the important difference that their young men could, by a simple act of volunteering, find access to arms. Little wonder that many should accordingly have joined the Waffen SS.

During 1941–43, very many did; sufficient to provide in March 1942 the manpower of a whole new division, 7th *Prinz Eugen*. Designated a mountain division, it was from the first committed to what perhaps was the most ferocious of all the campaigns fought in Europe in the Second World War – that between the Germans and their puppets and the Yugoslav partisans. Besides the division, Himmler recruited many older men of the Balkan *Volksdeutsche* into local anti-partisan police forces and later formed one of the last properly equipped panzergrenadier divisions, 18th *Horst Wessel*, from a fresh crop of youngsters.

By 1943, however, the initial enthu-

Above: Hitler and Quisling. *Below:* Mussert; the Dutch Nazi leader, with Himmler and Seyss-Inquart in Munich, 1941

Above : Himmler and Quisling inspect the SS Standarte Nordland. *Below :* Artur Axmann, Hitler Youth Leader, decorates young soldiers of the Hitler Jugend division, September 1944

siasm of the *Volksdeutsche* for Waffen SS had waned, probably as a result of their unhappy experience of what Germany's 'Greater Reich' policies meant in practice. Himmler, however, quite undeterred either by their reluctance to volunteer or by his own oft-stated insistence on the voluntary principle, instituted a programme of conscription throughout the Balkan lands and in that way brought in almost all fit racial Germans of military age. The effect was to increase the proportion of foreign-born members of the Waffen SS to more than a quarter of its total strength in 1943. The proportion would continue to rise.

An important factor contributing to this trend was the readiness shown by several nationalities in the conquered east to provide contingents. Foremost among them were the peoples of the Baltic Republics, Lithuanians, Latvians and Estonians, who, unlike the *Volksdeutsche*, had no claim to be accepted as German and, unlike the Scandinavians or Flemings, had not previously been regarded as 'kindred stock'. They had nevertheless good reasons for wishing to make common cause with Hitler, the most important of which was the history of their treatment at Russian hands. Long subject to the Tsars, their territories had been declared independent by Allied dictate in 1919 but in 1940 had been overrun by the Red Army and re-incorporated in the Russian Empire. Thus, to an even more marked extent than the Ukrainians, they had welcomed the Germans as liberators and had collaborated with them spontaneously.

There were Germans in positions of power who argued that Germany could exploit this situation to her advantage; that if the discontented minorities of the east were granted a measure of autonomy, the German army would profit thereby from the emergence of sizeable and dedicated allied armies, and her war industry from the willing co-operation of their national economies. Hitler would have none of it and the 'enlightened' policies of the 'eastern experts' accordingly collapsed. At a local level, however, the German armed forces did from the beginning of the campaign make use of native volunteers, both in labour and anti-partisan units, and the efficiency, often the ferocity, of the Baltic peoples attracted attention, eventually that of Himmler. His extermination squad commanders had found Latvian and Estonian volunteers to be among the most enthusiastic of their killers, while the higher SS police leaders reported well of the internal security units raised from the same source. Impressed on a tour of inspection by the Germanic appearance of a number of these men, he decided to press ahead with the formation of Waffen SS field units from Latvians and Estonians – though not from Lithuanians whose fervent Catholicism disqualified them in his eyes.

The first to be formed in early 1943 were, like the original West European groups, organised as legions of regimental, later brigade strength. Almost immediately afterwards it was decided to expand them into divisions, anything smaller having been found inadequate in fighting of the scale experienced on the eastern front. The 15th Latvian and 20th Estonian Divisions were accordingly added to the Waffen SS order of battle and in the following year the 19th Latvian (No 2).

By that stage, however, the same pattern of popular response already experienced by Waffen SS recruiting agents among the *Volksdeutsche* had begun to assert itself. An initial flood of recruits, sufficient to provide the nucleus of a self-supporting military structure, had dwindled to a trickle, and expansion and replacement could be sustained only by recourse to conscription. Once again this falling off was due to disillusionment, though provoked in this case by different factors. Estonian and Latvian political leaders had thought that their encouragement of their own young men to volunteer, providing as it did an earnest of their intentions to co-operate in Germany's plans for the east and to support her war effort, would be met by German assurances of a privileged future for their peoples. By 1944 no such assurances had been given by anyone who counted and the physical evidence indicated unmistakably that Hitler intended to treat the former Baltic Republics scarcely, if at all, better than any other part of his eastern conquests. By that stage, however, it was far too late for the Balts to retreat from the positions they had taken up. Russian re-occupation, now imminent, promised far worse than German indifference to their natural aspirations and these three Waffen SS divisions accordingly braced themselves to fight it out to the end. Two shared in the Wehrmacht's step-by-step retreat into the fatherland, the third formed part of Schörner's Army Group which the Red Army penned up in the Courland pocket of Latvia for the last nine months of the war. All suffered severely in the fighting and the survivors were sent to forced labour in Russian camps.

Heterogeneous though they were, these foreign units of the Waffen SS raised before 1943 were all composed of peoples for whom some place could be found, within Himmler's scheme of acceptable racial categories. It was true that many were by then conscripts, evidence of the fact that he had been forced to abrogate one of his two fundamental principles of recruitment to the order, but the second, which insisted on the exclusion of all non-Aryan stock, remained, at least in theory, intact. In the spring of that year, however, he took a crucial decision. So devouring had become his ambition to command an autonomous army, so demanding were the tasks which as supreme police authority he was called, in to discharge and so starved were his subordinates of men, that he authorised the enlistment, for

anti-partisan operations in Yugoslavia, of a Slav division. It was to be composed of that strange minority of Serbian Muslims, the descendants of those Christian mountaineers forcibly converted to Islam by the Turks in the middle ages, which lived in the former Austrian protectorate of Bosnia-Herzogovina.

But if the racial principle was to be breached, there were good reasons for choosing the Bosnians in doing so. The war with Tito's Serbian partisans was now assuming formidable dimensions and Himmler shared with the army much of the responsibility for waging it. The local *Volksdeutsche* could be brought to provide some of the necessary manpower but by no means all. The Bosnians, whose hatred for the Christian Serbs was bitter and mutual, offered an obvious supplement. They had made excellent soldiers in the old Austrian imperial army and now declared themselves more than ready to take on Tito's men, their traditional religious enemies whatever profession they made of communism. In February, 1943, therefore, the establishment of an SS Bosnian-Herzogovinian Mountain Division was announced and a vigorous recruiting programme instituted. By September the division was under training in France and by the beginning of 1944 had returned to Yugoslavia to undertake anti-partisan operations.

Himmler had resurrected for his new force, now entitled the 13th *Handschar* division many of the trappings and forms of the Muslim regiments of the old Austrian army. The men wore the fez, with the SS runes, were led in prayer by regimental imams and were in many cases commanded by former officers of the disbanded Habsburg units. Himmler had also secured the services of the Grand Mufti of Jerusalem as overseer of the division's religious practices. He, who can in no sense be compared either in personal or political terms with the striking Subhas Chandra Bose, had come nevertheless into much the same relationship with the Nazis. A refugee from British justice, which rightly held him responsible for the fomentation of anti-Jewish excesses in Palestine, he had been taken up by the Germans for their own purposes, but his incompetence and untrustworthiness made him of little use to them. Certainly if he had any influence in the Bosnian division, it can only have been for the bad, for it behaved unsatisfactorily wherever it was sent. After mutinying in France, a mutiny which the Mufti admittedly helped to quell, it steadfastly refused on its return to Yugoslavia to operate outside its own area, where it confined itself chiefly to massacring and pillaging the defenceless Christians. In late 1944, Himmler ordered its disbandment. He was also forced to disband, for the same reasons, the two other Muslim divisions, which, despite the warnings emitted by the behaviour of the first, he had raised during 1944. These were 21st *Skanderberg*, composed of Muslim Albanians

and 23rd *Kama*, the latter of much less than divisional size. The Muslim experiment, appealing though it must have been to Himmler who could fancy to have established through it some touch with the Turkmen hordes of his hero, Ghengis Khan, had proved a complete failure. The place of these divisions in the battle with Tito had to be taken by several from the German army, which Hitler could increasingly ill-spare.

The inadequacy of the Muslim divisions did not of course make itself apparent at once and in the interim Himmler, like a puritan who has taken up sin, authorised the establishment in April 1943 of a further Slav division. This was to be raised from the volunteers in the Ukraine, an area peopled by a race whose nationality defies accurate definition. Parts of its territory lie within Russia, whose government has always insisted on regarding

Danish volunteers disembark in Russia, June 1942

Above: Dutch SS men, 1941. *Below:* Waffen SS officer welcomes Dutch nurses volunteering for duty on the eastern front

the Ukrainians as Russian, though they claim a separate identity. Other parts are, or were before 1939, Polish but until 1918 had formed the Austrian province of Galicia. What was undoubted was that many Ukrainians had welcomed the German army as liberators and despite the indignities and sufferings inflicted by the invader were still willing to volunteer for his army as late as 1943. It was these that Himmler drew on to set up the 14th *Galizien* division, the title indicating that it was recruited exclusively from the old Habsburg province and so could be held to embody the traditions of a former German-speaking army. The deception fooled no one, probably not even Himmler, and since there was no way to distinguish Galician from non-Galician Ukrainians, the division in practice freely recruited

both. In action, to which it was unwisely committed in the east, it fought only once, was surrounded and fought its way free at such heavy cost that it had to be withdrawn from the front.

Had Himmler seized his chance in 1943, it seems probable that he might have found the manpower to fill out a series of Slav divisions. But by waiting to see how the first performed in action, however sensible a precaution as things turned out, he denied himself access to the Ukrainian recruiting area, which was overrun in the battle which destroyed the 14th Division. There remained, nevertheless, large reserves of Slav manpower in German hands, many of them formed into local security units, but the majority in prisoner-of-war camps. A number of the locally raised units, including two divisions of Cossacks who had deserted *en bloc*, were concentrated into *ad hoc* SS units and others were created by drafts on the populations of the puppet states of Hitler's empire, Hungary in particular. Three titular divisions of Hungarians, 25th, 26th and 33rd, were brought into being between the end of 1944 and May, 1945. Regiments, brigades and battlegroups were formed from such disparate groups as Caucasians, Turkmen, Bulgarians, Rumanians and Serbs, all racially beneath contempt had anyone cared to recall the provisions of the SS code at that stage of the war.

But the most promising source of recruitment in 1943–44, when some shreds of hope for a successful outcome still lingered, was in Russia itself, or rather in the Russian prisoner-of-war camps in Germany. The Germans had during the course of the eastern war captured rather more than four million Russian soldiers and though the majority had already died, by negligence, mistreatment or design, enough still lived to form, if they were willing, an enormous renegade army. The prospect enthused many 'enlightened' Nazis who believed that they had

found in General Vlasov, a captured deputy army group commander disillusioned by Stalinism, exactly the man to conjure it into being. With their backing, he set out in 1943 to convert the inmates of the camps to this new cause. Impeded by the opposition of the 'realists', who included Himmler, and lacking Hitler's firm approval, the project made slow progress. Not unnaturally, it did not recommend itself readily to the prisoners themselves, and less so the nearer the Red Army approached the borders of Germany. Nevertheless, since volunteering was often the only alternative to death by overwork and starvation, Vlasov had by the beginning of 1945 assembled the nucleus of his anti-communist army. To it were added the only two Russian divisions, 29th and 30th, which Himmler attempted to raise. Neither was larger than a regiment.

The fate of Vlasov's army was an extraordinary one: 'the Waffen SS were the only enemy it ever fought and the story is one of the queerest of the whole war'. Stationed outside Prague in May 1945, Vlasov was importuned by Czech resistance leaders to bring his Russians into the city to forestall its destruction by the Waffen SS garrison. He was moved to accede, perhaps by a calculation that an anti-Nazi demonstration now offered him and his soldiers their only hope of working their passage back. For several days they fought a running battle with the German garrison emplaced in the citadel and, at the approach of the Russians, made good their escape to the American demarcation line. By then, however, the Russians and the Western Allies had already agreed that no enemy soldiers should be allowed to cross from one zone to another to surrender and Vlasov's men were herded back towards the Red Army. He, his associates and many of the rest were subsequently executed. The same fate was

realities of German rule, itself an expression of the unwillingness of Hitler and the men around him, who alone counted in the making of policy, to modify their plans of domination. The West European SS, citizens of states with long-established traditions of independence, and a strong sense of national identity, represented no one but themselves and a few crackpot native Fascists. Their governments very sensibly chose to treat most of those who returned from the eastern front with lenience, rightly recognising that there was little civil imprisonment could do to reinforce the punishment they had received there.

Militarily, the contribution made by the foreign SS is more difficult to assess. The *Volkdeutsche* formed an important part of many of the better Waffen SS divisions, though the few raised from that source alone were of mediocre quality. The West European divisions, *Wiking* outstanding among them, performed consistently well, but their numbers counted for little in the scale of the fighting on the eastern front where they always fought. The Slav units, in almost every case, did not merit the time devoted or equipment given to them.

Their fighting record certainly cannot have added to Himmler's self-esteem, already bruised by his betrayal of principle in calling them into existence. Nor was their failure offset by the distinction earned by the Western European SS. By that stage of the war however, he had long put behind him the vision of the simple, sunny Aryan world he had dreamed of with Darré and it is doubtful whether he cared any longer of whom or what the SS comprised. The important thing was that it existed, that it grew in power and numbers and that what remained of Germany's institutions and conquests were falling progressively under its control.

meted out to the numerous *Osttruppen* who had fallen into British hands, and later returned to the east. The unhappiest of these episodes concerned the survivors of the SS Cossack Cavalry divisions who, with their families, forcibly resisted repatriation and compelled their British guards to kill a number of them before they were overcome.

The non-Germanic SS has attracted more attention than almost any other constituent part of Hitler's armed forces. Rightly so, in view of their numbers, which exceeded by the end of the war those of the native-born Germans under Himmler's control. The value of their contribution to Germany's war effort is however very dubious, whether measured in political or military terms. Politically, the status of the non-Germans as standard bearers of German-sponsored autonomy for the eastern minorities was hopelessly compromised by their fellow-countrymen's experience of the

Nordic twilight

The bulk of the foreign SS units were creations of the last eighteen months of the war and thus came into existence far too late to reverse the tide of events which by then was flowing so strongly against Germany. Yet though the numbers of élite SS divisions were not, and probably could not have been increased during these closing months, the role that they came to play in the battle for Germany grew consistently in importance. Above all was this true of the fighting in the west, in which the SS panzer divisions played a central relief in three of the major battles against the Allied Liberation Armies: Normandy, Arnhem and the Ardennes.

At the same time the Waffen SS continued to shoulder a disproportionate share of the fighting on the eastern front, a number of divisions, 9th *Hohenstauffen* and 10th *Frundsberg* in particular, managing to participate in three major battles, one in the east, two in the West, between April and September 1944. This was due to two factors: the 'first, that some Waffen SS formations, like *Wiking* and *Totenkopf*, had become the mainstay of the defence on certain Army Group fronts in Russian and grew more indispensable as the quality of the ordinary divisions declined; the second that Hitler had come to treat the élite Waffen SS as his special task force, to be committed whenever and wherever a situation had to be restored as a matter of urgency. As the relative strength of the German armed forces decreased, emergencies of that sort arose with gathering frequency and the élite Waffen SS panzer and panzer-grenadier divisions were uniquely fitted to deal with them. Highly mobile, which most ordinary divisions were not, equipped with a larger complement of armour than the army panzer divisions, composed of unusually tough, dedicated and skilful soldiers and led by the new breed of

SS infantrymen at rest during operations, September 1944

young but experienced commanders which the *Junkerschule* and the eastern battles had produced, they could be transferred at short notice from front to front along the not yet devastated railway system to intervene with powerful effect immediately on arrival. And that arrival was now not only welcomed but often prayed for by the hard-pressed commanders and soldiers of the German army, whose respect and confidence the best Waffen SS divisions had won in full measure. Indeed, whatever the distrust between Himmler and the High Command, relations between their subordinates had never been better than they were in early 1944. In the field, the Waffen SS had long ceased the effort to cultivate a separate identity and were glad to adopt, much to Himmler's disapproval, a traditionally military manner and outlook; in return, the army willingly accepted them as comrades, and even the highest commanders were ready to concede their expertise, if not quite their superiority, in the more desperate sort of operation.

A classic example of their skill in rescue operations is provided by accounts of the battle of Tarnopol in April, 1944. Since July of the previous year, when *Das Reich* and *Totenkopf* had spearheaded what was to prove almost the last successful counter-offensive of any scale against the Red Army, Germany's eastern front had been driven inexorably backward. The winter weather had imposed its usual restrictions on extended movement but with the coming of spring the southern wing of the Red Army had lurched forward, pinning Manstein's Army Group back against the Carpathians and encircling one of his armies, First Panzer, in what came to be called the Kamenets-Podolsk pocket. On the strength of the army were a number of SS units, the most sizeable *Leibstandarte*, recently returned from a mission to Italy where it had been sent to reinforce the German hold on the mainland follow-

Above: A Panther tank with SS panzer grenadiers aboard moves to the attack near Tilly, Normandy, June 28th 1944
Left: SS sharpshooters in Normandy

ing the Allied landings in Sicily. It, and indeed the whole Panzer Army was far too important a component of Hitler's dwindling armoured strength to be allowed to fall into Russian hands and he accordingly ordered the transfer of II SS Panzer Corps (*Hohenstauffen* and *Frundsberg*) from France to extricate it. In a fine display of mobile tactics it did so very briskly and was then withdrawn into strategic reserve in Poland. *Leibstandarte* was transported to Belgium to rest and re-equip.

Shortly before the conclusion of this successful operation, the veteran *Wiking* had also been surrounded on the lower Dneiper, with seven other divisions. In this case, the armoured task force available to Manstein was very much smaller and *Wiking*'s commander was told that his rescue

would depend largely on what efforts he himself could make to break out towards his rescuers. After a fortnight encircled, his units were in no proper shape to mount a co-ordinated breakout and the column was harried continuously by swarming Russian tanks. Degrelle, the Belgian commander of *Wallonian*, has left a harrowing account of its experiences: 'In this frantic race vehicles were overturned, throwing wounded in confusion to the ground. A wave of Soviet tanks overtook the first vehicles and caught more than half the convoy; the wave advanced through the carts, breaking them under our eyes, one by one like boxes of matches, crushing the wounded and the dying horses'. Though *Wiking* as an entity survived this disaster, it was to be several months before it was fit to fight again.

Meanwhile the western Wehrmacht was bracing itself for battle, which no German in France and Belgium deceived himself could be more than a few months in coming. How best that battle was to be fought, however, remained a matter of fierce debate, between the responsible German generals, Rundstedt, the Commander-in-Chief West, and Rommel, commander of Army Group B on the Channel coast. Both agreed that in their armoured divisions lay the best hope of repelling an Allied invasion but where and when those divisions were to be most effectively deployed they could not agree. Rommel, wary veteran of a dozen battles fought under the lethal eyes of a superior Allied air force, argued that the panzers could certainly not safely move any distance by day and it was therefore vital, if they were to intervene decisively, that they should be positioned as close to the beaches as possible, whatever sacrifices might have to be made in consequence to the venerable military principle of concentration of force. Rundstedt, whose battlefields had always been commanded from the air by the Luftwaffe, and who failed in consequence to

grasp how crippling contrary conditions could be, clung to convention. He argued, justifiably, that the first Allied landing might well prove a feint and that to commit the panzers against it would rob him of all flexibility should a second and more serious threat develop elsewhere on his long coastal front. He insisted therefore that the tanks must be held back and allowed to intervene only when the Allies had clearly shown their hand, though of course before they had had the chance to play it decisively. Since Rommel persisted in his view that Allied airpower would nail the panzers to the ground and keep them nailed long after Rundsdedt had made up his mind to move them, the dispute had to be referred for settlement to Hitler. He settled it on terms which pleased neither party, and which furthermore ensured that he would have the crucial say-so in the initial conduct of the battle. Some of the panzer divisions, he decided, should be positioned under Rommel's, some under Rundstedt's control. Rundstedt was to hold his back as he wanted to, but on the proviso that he should not move them without reference to OKW, Hitler's personal staff.

Two of the three divisions which Hitler has thus effectively reserved to his own use were Waffen SS, *Hitler Jugend* based in Normandy and *Leibstandarte* in Belgium. Another two of the remaining seven were also Waffen SS, 17th *Panzergrenadierdivision Gotz von Berlichingen*, stationed south of the Loire and *Das Reich*, stationed south of Bordeaux. These four divisions represented a disproportionate share of Panzer Group West's strength, since all were considerably stronger than their army counterparts, having six instead of four organic battalions of infantry, more artillery and, on average, a higher complement of tanks. But the importance of the SS element

An SS infantry officer among the debris of defeat, France, 1944

should not be measured solely in terms of comparison with the army panzer divisions, but must be seen in the context of German defensive capability as a whole. For as Hitler and the Allies alike recognised, the German infantry divisions would be of limited value in the coming battle. Numerous though they were (some fifty in all), the majority were so-called *bodenständige* units, that is equipped only for a static role. Moreover those positioned on the Mediterranean coast could not be used to reinforce a battle in the north, for fear of a secondary Allied landing there and, though the Allies were unaware of this, those guarding the Channel narrows were not to be transferred to Normandy until Hitler was convinced that the danger of an invasion via the Pas de Calais would not materialise. In short, the invasion battle would have to be fought by those infantry divisions immediately to hand and by such other units as could be transferred quickly into the danger area – which meant the panzer divisions. Of the nine available (for one was to be left in the south) the SS provided four. Shortly after the battle began, it was to add another two (*Hohenstauffen* and *Frundsberg*). In a very real sense then, Normandy was to be an SS battle.

Because of the success of the Allied deception plan, the German armour intervened generally too late on D-Day itself to prevent the first waves securing a foothold. But in the operations designed by the Allies to enlarge their bridgehead and eventually to break out into open country, it was most often the SS divisions which they found barring their path. From the point of view of the Allied generals, they were glad that it should be so, since their strategy was to engage and 'write down' the German armour on the British front while the Americans built up their strength for an unhindered drive into Brittany. For the Allied soldiers on the ground, which meant chiefly the British east

Gustav von Kahr, Prime Minister of
Bavaria 1923. Hitler's unwilling ally

Otto Skorzeny, rescuer of Mussolini
and SS commando extraordinary

and west of Caen, that strategy, and
the opposition it attracted, was to
mean a series of bitter, protracted
and often apparently fruitless killing-
matches.

The first of these battles was that
for the crossings of the river Odon,
south-east of Caen, planned as a conventional infantry attack but supported by artillery and armour in
great strength. Beginning well on
26th June, the Scottish division which
acted as spearhead quickly opened a
corridor as far as the river but soon
found itself taken concentrically in
flank by Dietrich's I SS Panzer Corps
(*Leibenstandarte* and *Das Reich*).
Forced to halt in its tracks, it suffered
on the fourth day a devastating
counter-attack by II SS Panzer Corps
(*Frundsberg* and *Hohenstauffen*) and
had to call the operation off.

Hohenstauffen and *Frundsberg*, whose
intervention conformed to what by
now was a classic pattern for the SS,
had mounted their assault almost
straight off the line of march. Having
left France only in April to deliver
their counterstroke at Tarnopol, they
had been ordered back to the west on
12th June and had arrived on the

border on 16th July. Just as Rommel
had predicted, however, the vigilance
of the Allied air patrols and the
destruction wrought by bombing on
the French railway system had caused
them to spend almost a fortnight on
the short journey from Alsace-
Lorraine to Normandy. It was a
remarkable tribute to their morale
and march-discipline that they should
have arrived so combat-fit.

Das Reich had also had to make a
long and trying journey to reach the
battle, moving north from Bordeaux
by road, but its behaviour *en route*
calls for different judgement. Harried
by resistance fighters, it was unable
to get on at the speed it would have
liked and at Oradour-sur-Glane, a
village chosen apparently arbitrarily
by one of the regimental commanders,
it halted to inflict reprisals. The men
of the village were rounded up and
shot, the women and children herded
into the church, which was set on fire.
All but one of the 642 inhabitants
perished. This atrocity, by far the
most terrible committed in western
Europe by any German formation,
passed unnoticed at the time. *Das
Reich* itself was swallowed up im-

Anton Mussert, leader of the Dutch Nazi party

mediately afterwards in the fighting in the perimeter of the bridgehead.

Within three weeks of the Odon battle *Leibstandarte*, *Hohenstauffen* and *Hitler Jugend* were to be instrumental in blunting what thereto was the most concentrated attempt by Allied armour to break out of the Caen pocket. Codenamed Goodwood, this operation unleashed on 18th July three strong British armoured divisions in a straight run down the corridor between Caen and the heights to its east in an attempt to break clear over the Bourgebus ridge at its end and out into open country. It was preceded by the most devastating carpet bombardment yet laid by the Allied airforces on ground positions in Normandy, a three-hour earthquake which left the German infantry trembling incapably and most of the tanks deployed by the supporting army panzer division disabled or destroyed. Following headlong in its wake, the British divisions achieved all their primary objectives on schedule but as the leading Shermans, undergunned and inflammable, reached the foot of Bourgebus ridge, squadron after squadron burst into flame. The crest was held in strength by Mark IV and Panther tanks of *Leibstandarte*, which had escaped the bombing. By next day they had been joined by elements of *Hitler Jugend* and *Hohenstauffen*. Once again Montgomery was forced, principally because of the resistance offered by Waffen SS units, to close down a major offensive operation.

Time, however, was running out for the whole of the German army in Normandy. Under-supplied and virtually unreinforced, except by driblets of infantry who could not stand up to the weight of the Allied attack, it was steadily succumbing to the attrition strategy of the Allies. Five days after the failure of Goodwood, the Americans on the opposite flank found the force to break through the thinning crest of the German defence and streamed south into open country. As one column made ground towards Avranches on the coast, another began an enveloping movement around the broken end of the German front at St-Lo. Encirclement threatened. The moment had come, by any rational military calculation, to order a withdrawal from Normandy to more defensible positions across the Seine.

That was not Hitler's view. He had always – at Moscow, at Stalingrad, at Sevastapol – insisted that his troops should fight 'to the last man and the last round' and he was not prepared to relax that principle now. His reasons were not wholly without substance. Once the western army abandoned its positions, he argued, it would expose itself to destruction on the same scale as the eastern army had risked in 1941, because it lacked the means to cover its retreat. The army, in short, was too weak to withdraw.

Its armoured component, he decided on the other hand, was still strong enough to mount a counterattack, which might yet prove decisive. The American breakout was still confined to a narrow corridor, commanded on one flank by the Germans, on the

117

Quisling contemplates his future, 1944

General von Lossow, Commander of the Bavarian division of the Reichsheer 1923. Hitler believed his soldiers would not fire on him

Walter Darré, whose beliefs in 'Blood and Soil' Himmler tried to embody in the SS marriage laws

other by the sea. If the panzer divisions were massed and launched in a body towards the coast at Avranches, they might sever the head of the American armoured column from its tail, defeat it in detail and turn to devastate the beach-heads.

During the first week of August, therefore, the opening moves in a cloud-cuckoo game of strategy were played out in western Normandy. While the American armoured and motorised columns drove hard for the east in an ever more menacing curve, the German panzer divisions – *Leibstandarte, Das Reich, Hohenstauffen, Frundsberg, Gotz von Berlichingen* and the army's 2nd, 21st and 116th, moved west on an inner arc. On the morning of 7th August they unleashed their attack.

To describe the outcome as a fiasco is to misrepresent by understatement. The Mortain counterattack was a disaster on the largest scale, leading directly to the destruction of the German western army. Its failure can be blamed on none of the divisions taking part, which fought with great tenacity, *Leibstandarte* and *Das Reich* actually succeeding in penetrating the Americans' open flank. None, however, any longer disposed of the power to develop an attack in depth. The failure was a function of Hitler's folly; within a week he was to pay the price of it.

That he was spared paying in full was due to the extraordinary exertions of the youngest – in every sense – of the élite SS Panzer Divisions, *Hitler Jugend*. Left to bolster the infantry divisions opposite the British when the rest of the panzers had gone west a week earlier, it found itself on 13th August holding the last exit from Normandy open to the Germans. This, the Falaise-Argentan gap, represented the neck of a sack whose sides were being drawn tight to the north by the British and Canadians attacking from Caen, to the south by the Americans now streaming freely past the halted German armour at Mortain and racing towards the Seine. Within the sack the remnants of over twenty German infantry and eight armoured divisions were struggling for their lives. For the next six days *Hitler Jugend* fought to hold open their escape-route. On 20th August, reduced to a mere skeleton, it was forced to yield up the effort. By then, however, as many of the men of the trapped divisions who could still move, though almost none of their equipment had been got back to the line of the Seine.

They had been got back almost without reference to Hitler, who continued to demand the impossible, by the new commander of Army Group B whom he had appointed on 16th August, the 'fireman of the eastern front', General Model. He, who in July had restored the line in Poland after the catastrophic battle known – so large was its scale and so fluid its form – simply as the Destruction of Army Group Centre, was perhaps the only man with nerve enough to have acted independently. Kluge, the wounded Rommel's successor, had lacked the nerve even to tell Hitler the facts, and Dietrich, his old bodyguard, still his favourite and, as commander of I SS Panzer Corps, an eye-witness of the disaster, refused to do so for him. 'If I want to get shot, that's the way to do it,' he had told Kluge. Model had come, seen, accepted the defeat for what it was and picked up the pieces that remained.

In the circumstances, he had behaved with extraordinary moral courage, for August 1944 was a bad month for generals to cross Hitler, even over trifles. Only a month before, the 'military opposition', dormant for so long that Allied intelligence may be excused for having doubted its existence, had tried to kill him. The failure of the attempt, and the even more inept failure of its *coup d'état* in Berlin, had unstoppered all Hitler's latent hatred and contempt for the military caste, and he had given himself over to an orgy of revenge.

Model's near-insubordination escaped retribution perhaps only because of its effrontery.

The treachery of the generals might have been arranged by Himmler, so perfectly did it serve to further his ambitions. For it resulted at a personal level, in his own appointment to the crucial post of commander of the Reserve Army, which carried with it control over the allocation of manpower and equipment (henceforth in consequence the Waffen SS was to lack for little); and, more generally, in the preferment of Waffen SS over army officers for positions of command. Hitherto, the highest rank which any SS officer had held was corps commander (though Hausser had exercised control of Seventh Army for a short period); shortly there were to be SS Army and even Army Group commanders and a titular SS Army would be formed. No matter that these were commands in a Wehrmacht moving inescapably towards defeat; with Himmler, forms counted for a great deal more than reality.

Hitler's growing dependence on the Waffen SS was reinforced by the part its divisions were to play in halting the Allied Liberation Army's exploitation of its victory in Normandy. That exploitation had carried the British vanguards by early September to within striking distance of the German border and, after much heart-searching, Eisenhower had given Montgomery permission to complete his victory by establishing an airborne bridgehead across the Rhine at Arnhem. The drop was organised with complete success but Allied intelligence had failed to detect that *Hohenstauffen* and *Frundsberg*, battered almost out of recognition by their long ordeal and subsequent flight, had been sent to Arnhem to rest. Alerted within hours of the landing, what tanks and infantry remained to them were at once committed to battle against the outmatched parachutists of the British 1st Airborne Division The key to the battle was the Arnhem

road bridge, which had been seized by an airborne battalion with orders to hold it until the British armoured columns arrived from the south. To stop them, and to overcome the American parachutists holding open the crossings of the rivers below the Rhine, *Hohenstauffen* and *Frundsberg* had themselves to secure passage across it, since all their tanks were on its north bank. For four days, therefore, a bitter battle raged around the northern end of the bridge until, overwhelmed by superior numbers and weight of equipment, the remnants of the parachute battalion surrendered. They had held out twice as long as planned; but the British armour had made only half the distance expected in the time. 'Thus it was that three hours before the first British tank crossed the Nijmegen bridge, heading north, the first German tank crossed the Arnhem bridge, heading south.' The result was decisive for the outcome of the operation.

While the British were failing to break into Germany by the northern route, Patton's Third American Army which had closed the ring round the German Army in Normandy, was battering equally fruitlessly in the south at the Lorraine gateway. Whether it should or should not have been accorded the priority in supplies which Montgomery had won from Eisenhower for the Arnhem operation remains a matter of bitter dispute. But the argument that it would, if so favoured, have broken the West Wall at a single blow must be treated with caution. It is true that Germany's western army had been devastated in the battle of Normandy and its flight from France, but from its remnants the High Command, with a talent peculiarly German, had organised by early September a remarkably cohesive frontier guard. Typical of its expertise in improvising 'alarm units',

as they were called, was that formed for the defence of Metz, Division No 462, one of whose best battalions consisted of the staff and students of the SS signal school located there. It, and the quickly refurbished *Gotz von Berlichingen*, steadfastly defended the old fortifications against heavy and protracted assaults by Patton's much superior force.

Defeated in Holland and stalemated in Lorraine, the Allies had lost by October the impetus which had carried them from France to the German border in a headlong gallop during September. The autumn fighting soon resolved itself into a bitter battle of attrition, which in the long run Germany could not sustain but from which the Allies could not go over to the offensive until the onset of better weather and the organisation of a more productive supply system. By early December, therefore, plans for bringing Germany to defeat in the open field had been deferred to the spring.

Hitler, however, was not prepared to acquiesce in this timetable. He could read the signs of impending annihilation as well as the Allied intelligence officers but still had the will, and was finding the means, to upset these calculations. During the later autumn he had raised a large number of so-called *Volksgrenadier* divisions and with these and the re-equipped panzer divisions planned to mount a major spoiling attack against one or other of his enemies. A quick appreciation convinced him that his striking force would be swallowed up if committed to the eastern front. He judged the west more vulnerable, for two reasons, one political, the other military. Politically, he thought the Allies might be brought to sue for terms if hit hard enough, leaving him only with the Russians to fight; militarily, he believed he could manage the sort of blow which would collapse the Allied will to fight. It would, like the 1940 attack, be launched through the Ardennes, have as its geographical

121

Peiper advances on Malmedy, where he was to organise the massacre of American prisoners, December 1944

objective the channel coast near Antwerp and as its strategic object the separation of the British from the American armies.

His generals attempted to persuade him of the objections to this plan: that its aims were over-ambitious and that its failure would cost him his last uncommitted reserve. Hitler was adamant, advancing much the same argument as he had done in the dispute over the conduct of the battle of Normandy: in brief, that Germany was now too weak not to attack. And to ensure that the attack would be driven home with resolution, he confided command of the principal elements involved to a Waffen SS officer, his old comrade Sepp Dietrich.

His command, the Sixth SS Panzer Army (the first unit of so large a size to be designated SS) was to consist of five infantry and four armoured divisions, *Leibstandarte* and *Hitler Jugend* in the first wave, with *Das Reich* and *Hohenstauffen* as the follow-up. All had been lavishly re-equipped with the Mark V Panther in the divisional panzer battalions and with ninety Tigers under central control. On the left of Dietrich's Army, the Fifth Panzer had the mission of guarding its flank and deepening and widening the break-in, but the principal and decisive role was his: to break through to Antwerp, ninety miles from his start line.

This was to be the last great attack of the SS, indeed of the German Army. It was one which the young soldiers of the SS divisions had been told, and believed, they would win. 'I write during one of the momentous hours before the attack,' a letter from a lieutenant of *Hitler Jugend* to his sister reads, 'full of excitement and expectation of what the next days will bring. Some believe in living but

life is not everything! It is enough to know that we attack and will throw the enemy from our homeland. It is a holy task. Above me is the terrific noise of V-1s and artillery, the voice of war'. The same morning, 16th December, his division moved forward to the assault.

The American divisions opposite, overstretched and unprepared, were in many cases panicked into precipitate flight by the quite unexpected arrival of the Panthers and Tigers, which they usually lacked the weapons to engage, in their forward positions. On Fifth Panzer Army's front, therefore, the 2nd Panzer and Panzer *Lehr* divisions were able to make a quick and rapid penetration. In Dietrich's sector, however, which was the one which counted, his armoured spearheads, after a promising start, ran up against firm resistance which continued to stiffen. This was due in part to the nature of the terrain, which favoured the de-

fence and made fast armoured movement difficult, but also to the devotion of the American infantry divisions in *Leibstandarte*'s and *Hitler Jugend*'s path. Their will to fight was very much strengthened after 17th December by the rapidly disseminated news that the SS were killing their prisoners; and such indeed had been the fate of the first to fall into the hands of the leading battle group of *Leibstandarte*, for the battle group commander, Peiper, had ninety of them machine-gunned in a meadow outside the town of Malmedy. His reasons have never satisfactorily been explained, though they had probably something to do with the orders given to spread 'a wave of terror' ahead of the advance. The orders were certainly not intended to be interpreted as they were by Peiper, and the effect of his actions was in any case counter-productive.

The results achieved by the formation specifically detailed to spread alarm and confusion, the SS Colonel Otto Skorzeny's 'Trojan Horse' Brigade were on the other hand spectacular. His two thousand commandos, many former emigrants to America who spoke English fluently, and all turned out in American uniforms, caused serious interruptions to the communications systems, destroyed a good deal of equipment and stores and raised panic in places as far distant as Eisenhower's headquarters, which was put under special guard on the rumour that a picked team of assassins was on its way to kill the Supreme Commander.

But neither Skorzeny's high jinks nor Peiper's terror methods could materially alter the balance of advantage which, though it had seemed to swing the Germans' way in the first few days of the campaign, had returned sharply to the Allies by 24th December. By then the army panzer divisions, though not the SS had advanced sixty miles but were at their last gasp. Over Christmas the weather, which had prevented flying, cleared and the Allied airforces, working in concert with strong ground reinforcements, began to bustle the Germans briskly back to whence they had come.

With the failure of the Ardennes offensives Hitler's long run on the stage of ground strategy may be judged over. He still of course retained the power to make his own soldiers do his will, which meant that they must fight it out to the finish, but he had lost the means to impose his will on the enemy. In the four months of war which remained he was never again to launch an attack which would seriously trouble any major commander on either front. This is not to say that his troops henceforth were to be committed to a wholly passive defence. Attack they would: but with objectives which even Hitler himself recognised as limited.

The most important of these limited offensives was again to be an SS affair and one which would unite the largest number of the elite German and Germanic divisions ever assembled for one operation. It was designed to restore the situation in central Hungary, from which Hitler was drawing his last supplies of natural oil produced by the wells around Lake Balaton. Threatened by the southern wing of the Red Army, which in January had overwhelmed the SS garrison of Budapest, this region Hitler decided in February must be secured by strong counteroffensive. *Wiking* and *Totenkopf* were already in the area; to join them he sent the battered Sixth SS Panzer Army (*Leibstandarte, Das Reich, Hohenstauffen, Hitler Jugend*), and other units including 16th *Reichsführer SS*. For all their force, they could however do little against the enormously superior numbers of the Russians and though, between the first and third weeks of March they did succeed in winning some ground, it had all to be surrendered when the

Himmler and Reich Youth Leader Axmann inspect volunteers 1943

enemy recovered his balance and struck back.

By the beginning of April, defeat stared Hitler and his soldiers in the face. Many would have accepted it then and there, provided that they they could be guaranteed British or American captivity, but Hitler was determined to go on to the end. Very few wished to join him. Certainly not Himmler, to whom he had done no kindness, and himself no good, by appointing him commander of the Vistula Army Group in late January. Fascinated though the Reichsführer had been by military panoply all his life, he had, and soon found that he had, no talent at all for command. Worse, he concluded that the war itself was lost and yielding to the promptings of his self-appointed foreign policy advisers, began to open communications with the Allies.

These were not, and would not have been, entertained but in any case came far too late. By mid-April the fronts in the east and west had both collapsed, Germany was about to be cut in two and Berlin itself was threatened with siege.

In these last moments, Hitler announced plans for the operation which would 'inflict the greatest and bloodiest defeat in their history' on the Russians. It was to be mounted by the three armies nearest Berlin, of which Steiner's was to play the chief part. This was the Steiner who had commanded a battalion in the original *Leibstandarte*; now a full General, his Command had recently included *Frundsberg, Polizei, Nordland, Neder-*

Below: Himmler, Hitler and Sepp Dietrich play generals, 1939. **Right:** Mussert, Himmler, Schwarz and Wolff

Left: Alfred Rosenberg, Minister for the Occupied East, whose racial theories were used to indoctrinate the SS. *Above:* Degrelle, the Belgian Fascist leader, preaches the gospel of Nazism, Brussels, 1943

land and *Wallonien* but most had since been scattered. He was nevertheless ordered to press home the attack and much of Hitler's last, crazed days in the bunker under the Reich Chancellery, beneath the spot where the boots of the *Leibstandarte* had crashed to salute the comings and goings of a dozen years before, were spent in following the imagined progress of his skeleton army.

Hitler's recognition of the failure of Steiner's attack and his discovery of Himmler's double-dealing, which occurred over the days of 22nd-23rd April, are generally accepted as marking the moment when he de-cided to make an end of things. The Waffen SS and its leaders had failed him. There was now no one he could trust, as he told his fellow tomb-dwellers, and he determined to die. While a handful of foreign volunteers of *Nordland, Charlemagne* and the 15th Latvian fought it out with the Russians in the ruins overhead, he completed the preparations for his suicide. He had already dismissed Himmler from all his posts and ordered the arrest of Göring, who had too eagerly invoked the provisions appointing him successor. Now he wrote his will, drafted his political settlement, married his mistress and made his farewells. On the afternoon of 30th April, he retired and shot himself. His body and that of his bride, who had joined him in suicide, were carried into the shell-torn garden of the Reich Chancellery by officers of his SS escort, and burned.

Soldiers like other soldiers?

Eight days after Hitler had been carried to a makeshift grave by his SS pall-bearers, the surviving representatives of the German High Command signed terms of unconditional surrender with the Allies. Fifteen days after that, Himmler, a prisoner in British hands, swallowed poison and died. The myrmidons of his order had followed him in flight, some more successfully to safety in neutral lands, others to find obscurity and a new identity within Germany itself, the majority to be caught like him in the tightly drawn cordon of Allied control posts. The soldiers of such Waffen SS formations as still retained their cohesion had, at the express injunction of the German High Command, marched into the Allied lines and given themselves up.

It was a hang-dog end to an army which, Himmler had long before assured his confident, Kersten, would, like the Goths at Vesuvius, die round their chief rather than strike their standards. But since he had signally failed to prove himself a Gothic chieftain, it was not a surprising one. Nor is it surprising, in view of Himmler's abject behaviour in defeat and sordid, self-inflicted death in captivity, that 'in the Germany of today there is no SS legend of any serious consequence'. But then there are few historical legends in Germany today and none of the Nazi past, which

SS security troops of a mountain unit move off on an anti-partisan operation in the Yugoslav mountains, February 1944

lies as a barrier of over-charged silence between the young and the middle-aged. The questions are unasked, the answers unspoken.

It is outside Germany that the Nazi legend persists and most strongly in the lands of the victors, not of the occupied. And there surely there is an SS legend. It is a many-sided legend. Those parts of it which deal with systematic sadism and industrialised death exert the sort of guilty fascination from which the healthy-minded recoil and the pornographers have learn how to profit. Those which underlie serious attempts to explain the workings of the Nazi regime in terms of an SS 'state within a state' provide the material for an important debate between historians of contemporary Europe. But parallel to those there is another part to the legend, one of broader and not wholly distasteful appeal: that of the janissaries of the Waffen SS, faithful unto death and fiercer in combat than any soldiers who fought on western battle-

fields. It is a legend blemished by a record of known atrocities but one in which the ruthlessness and cruelty of individuals seem transcended by corporate dedication, comradeship and courage of unique degree. What truth is there in this legend? Were the Waffen SS a new army of janissaries? Were they also, as the prosecution charged at Nuremberg, criminals in uniform? Or were they simply, as Paul Hausser argued from the witness stand, soldiers like other soldiers?

The last they were certainly not, for a variety of reasons. Some are obvious. Others remain almost unperceived, perhaps because the significance of the form which Hitler gave to the German army when he inaugurated its re-expansion in 1935, has largely escaped observers. That form, deliberately chosen by Hitler, was that of a truly national army, something which Germany had never possessed before. The Kaiser's army had been an amalgam of the armies of the German states, which, unified though they had

Above left: SS assault gun in a defensive position on the Zhitomiv-Kiev road, December 1942. *Above:* Flemish Hitler Youths under inspection by an SS officer, April 1944. *Below:* An SS armoured column in action in Budapest, 1945

The destruction of the Warsaw Ghetto. The SD man in the right foreground has recently been identified and arrested

been in 1871, never quite ceased, like the states to which they had previously owed loyalty, to retain the marks of their disparate origins. The Bavarian army remained in fact a separate organisation until 1918 and even under Weimar the Bavarian division of the Reichswehr could strike an independent line in national affairs. And the semi-autonomous status of the individual regiments of the Empire was a factor which Berlin had always had to take into account in its dealings with the army. No cadet could be commissioned until he had been elected to membership of the regiment which he wished to join by its corps of officers, while they in turn felt a strong and reciprocated bond of 'club feeling' with former officers promoted to general rank. Some regiments, the Third Foot Guards for example, were particularly well represented on the General Staff, but all

Latvian SS volunteers made prisoner by the British, June 1945

had a distinct regimental identity which for better or worse determined their place in the military hierarchy. It may well be argued that this system was pernicious one, since election to the regiment and that regiment's allotment of position in the army's 'pecking order' were both a function of social status, and as such made for a snob-ridden officer corps. But the effect of the system was not wholly without merit, politically or militarily. Politically, it ensured that the army's organisation mirrored, and so kept touch with, the country's social system; militarily, it stimulated a highly competitive spirit between regiments, both in peace and, more important, in war. But above all, it made for a very independent army governed by its own arcane and highly complex code and jealous of the preservation of its traditions and variety. It goes without saying, that it was a supremely loyal army, but its loyalty had a fixed limit, determined by the dictates of self-preservation. Thus it

remained unswervingly loyal to the Kaiser – up to the moment when his insistence on retaining his throne forced the generals to choose between him and the army's dissolution. In that crisis they chose to put the army before their oath on the colours, though as it happened they had left things too late. But their choice is an indication of their fundamental attitude.

The reduction of the army by the terms of the Treaty of Versailles to a strength of 100,000 men entailed of course the scrapping of its traditional organisation, but Seeckt, the architect of the new Reichswehr and the archetype of the imperial officer, took steps to ensure that when these restrictions on its size were lifted, it should re-emerge from the carapace in its original form. Thus each of the new regiments was deemed 'tradition-bearer' of several of the old, which its offspring would in the future, it was intended, bring to life once more. They meanwhile sought to restrict their intake of officers to social types who would have been acceptable to the parent regiments. The ninth Regiment of the Reichswehr, for example, 'Graf Neun' ('Earl Nine') preserved the traditions of the Foot Guards and recruited a high proportion of its officers from traditionally military families of the Prussian nobility.

Now the 'Seeckt System' was anathema to Hitler, partly because he loathed and despised the old officer corps, partly because he had a very sensible fear of how indigestible a large army remade in its image might prove in a Nazi state. When he decided that the moment had come to risk re-expanding the Reichswehr, therefore, he would have no truck with the 'tradition-bearer' idea. The new German army was to be as uniform and monolithic an organisation as he could make it, one unit having to stand in exactly the same relationship to others as all the rest, and their officers, far from choosing each other,

being left in no doubt that they owed their commission as well as their loyalty to the Führer alone.

But what he succeeded in producing was a half-way house of an army, as efficient in combat as the Kaiser's had ever been, indeed even more tenacious in disaster, but one ambivalent in its loyalties and uncertain of its traditions. Röhm, in a sense had been right; a Nazi state needed a Nazi army, 'something new, fresh and unused', and that the Wehrmacht never became.

The Waffen SS on the other hand was unequivocally Nazi from the start. Its loyalty was never in question, but what is interesting is that on so firm an ideological foundation Himmler should have chosen to build in a form which owed a great deal to the imperial past. Two features predominated: rigorous selection and very strong unit identity.

The criteria of selection were, of course, quite different from those imposed in the Kaiser's army, having no regard at all to a candidate's social origins, but the effect was identical. An officer of the *Leibstandarte* may not have had to undergo the processes of election, but the inflexible standards of the racial, physical and ideological tests which he had to satisfy, would leave him with a strong sense of pre-election – in its way an even more powerful reinforcement of his confidence in his standing than election by his fellows would produce.

Perhaps even more important was the decision to confer powerfully evocative titles on the units, since that did most to ensure that the Waffen SS would have a superior *esprit de corps* and stronger popular appeal than the humdrum units of the army. *Leibstandarte, Totenkopf, Hohenstauffen!* These were names which rang with the excitement of battle and caught echoes of the panache of the past, of the Bodyguards of the Bavarian Kings, of the Death's Head Hussars of Frederick the Great, of the

BADGES OF THE SCHUTZSTAFFELN DIVISIONS

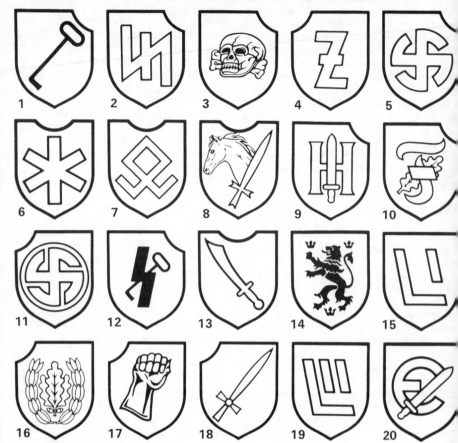

1 I SS Panzer Division 'Leibstandarte'	**11** XI SS Frw Pz Gren Division 'Nordland'
2 II SS Panzer Division 'Das Reich'	**12** XII SS Panzer Division 'Hitlerjugend'
3 III SS Panzer Division 'Totenkopf'	**13** XIII SS Mountain Division 'Handschar'
4 IV SS Pz Gren Division 'Polizei Division'	**14** XIV SS Waffen Gren Division 'Galizische No I'
5 V SS Panzer Division 'Wiking'	**15** XV SS Waffen Gren Division 'Latvian No I'
6 VI SS Mountain Division 'Nord'	**16** XVI SS Pz Gren Division 'Reichsführer SS'
7 VII SS Vol Mnt Division 'Prinz Eugen'	**17** XVII SS Pz Gren Division 'Gotz von Berlichingen'
8 VIII SS Cavalry Division 'Florian Geyer'	**18** XVIII SS Vol Pz Gren Division 'Horst Wessel'
9 IX SS Panzer Division 'Hohenstaufen'	**19** XIX SS Waffen Gren Division 'Latvian No II'
10 X SS Panzer Division 'Frundsberg'	**20** XX SS Waffen Gren Division 'Estonian No I'

21	XXI Waffen Geb Div der SS 'Skanderbeg'
22	XXII SS Frw Kav Division 'Maria Theresa'
23	XXIII SS Vol Pz Gren Division 'Nederland'
24	XXIV SS Waffen Mountain Div 'Karstjäger'
25	XXV SS Waffen Gren Division 'Hungarian No II'
26	XXVI SS Waffen Gren Division 'Hungarian No III'
27	XXVII SS Vol Gren Division 'Flemish No I'
28	XXVIII SS Vol Pz Gren Division 'Wallonie'
29	XXIX SS Waffen Gren Division 'Italian No I'
30	XXX SS Waffen Gren Division 'Russian No II'
31	XXXI SS Frw Gren Division
32	SS Frw Gren Division 'Böhmen-Mähren'
33	XXXII SS Vol Gren Division 'January 30'
34	XXXIII SS Waffen Gren Division 'Charlemagne'
35	XXXIV SS Gren Division 'Landstorm Nederland'
36	XXXV SS Pol Gren Division 'Polizei Division II'
37	XXXVI SS Waffen Gren Division 'Dirlewanger'
38	XXXVII SS Vol Cavalry Division 'Lützow'
39	XXXVIII SS Pz Gren Division 'Nibelungen'

regiments of the proprietorial colonels which had won honours in a dozen European wars. Little wonder that eager German youths should have competed for selection and, once enrolled, taken the fiercest pride in the reputation of divisions which bore such splendid titles into battle. Thus it was they, bearers though they were of a quite novel tradition, who most fully inherited the emotional legacy of the past; and their performance in combat demonstrates how powerful a hold these historical emotions retained in the German military mind – as indeed they still do. The modern Bundeswehr, an army 'new, fresh and unused' if ever there was one, casts back longing glances at the traditions of the Imperial Army, with whose regiments it constantly hankers to identify its own.

Himmler's decision to invoke the past in the service of the present, splendidly successful though it proved in practice, carried with it the risk of stimulating the same sort of institutional attitudes, which in the crisis of November 1918 had led the army to bring down the Kaiser. These attitudes, or rather the pattern of behaviour to which they rise, is usually called Praetorianism, a reference to the Roman Praetorian Guard's habit of making and breaking Caesars. Praetorianism is a phenomenon to which any state maintaining a standing army exposes itself, but the dictatorial state, which bases its rule on force, more than others. Most at risk are those regimes in which all power is vested in a single individual or groups of individuals, who are forced in consequence to maintain between themselves and the ruled a physical barrier of armed and picked men. The essential dilemma of the resulting situation has long been recognised, has indeed been epitomised in one of the most famous of Latin tags, '*Quis custodiet ipsos custodes?*'. Who indeed shall guard the guards? Not the ruler, since he paradoxically is their hostage. Nor

again an inner guard, since it will automatically inherit the life-and-death powers of the first. The problem is of course insoluble.

Hitler never solved it because he never had to face it, having the luck to be able to defer a conflict with the army until after the war had begun but before the Waffen SS, in whom Praetorian status was clearly latent had achieved the strength, and its leaders the confidence, to confront him directly. Thereafter both the army and the Waffen SS were so heavily and continuously engaged on

Nazi 'auxiliary' policemen in training
in Berlin, 1934

and beyond the frontiers of Germany
that Hitler could operate from the
centre without fear of attack by any
force larger than one which his
personal police escort could defeat. It
appears, and was, an extraordinarily
precarious position for a dictator to
tolerate, but nevertheless the truth
is that the principal impediment to
the plans of the July plotters was the
almost total absence of troops both
from the vicinity of the Wolf's Lair at
Rastenburg and from Berlin. The
success of their coup therefore turned
on their ability to mobilise the staff

of an armoured warfare school three
hour's drive from the city and, meanwhile, to block signal traffic between
Führer Headquarters and the capital
by deceit and bluff. When signal traffic
was restored before the troops could
arrive, the coup failed. The conspira-
tors were nevertheless overcome by
the smallest imaginable force, a
single battalion of security guards
whose commander remained loyal to
Hitler.

To Himmler's chagrin, the battalion belonged to the Army, not the Waffen SS. What debts of gratitude might he have incurred had he had the foresight to leave a battalion of the *Leibstandarte* in permanent garrison at Berlin! But the city was even emptier of Waffen SS than of army troops on 20th July 1944, a result of Hitler's – and Himmler's – decision, that their wartime role must be to win distinction at the front in order to fit them for a peace-time role as guardians of the regime.

Even at the end, when Himmler's loyalty to the Führer at last began to fray, he appears not to have considered using the Waffen SS as a counter in the game he was playing, principally because he was too woolly-minded to decide whether or not he was opposing Hitler but also because, as he would have recognised had he thought about it, his divisions were too deeply committed at the front to be disengaged. From first to last, therefore, the Waffen SS never approached the status of a Praetorian Guard, nor were they reckoned one by Hitler or Himmler.

But if not that, were they markedly better soldiers than those of the Wehrmacht? Do they deserve to be thought of as a new army of janissaries?

There is no simple answer to this question. Certainly it is true that some of the SS divisions performed superbly and consistently well; but that cannot be said of all. The lower-grade divisions, those underprivileged in the allotment of manpower or equipment, like the cavalry divisions, *Polizei* and the racial German formations, have an erratic record, even though as a consequence of their dubious quality, they were never commissioned to undertake tasks of a really demanding nature. *Polizei*, for

example, began the war as an undisguisedly over-age and under-equipped body, was always allotted run of the mill duties and even after it had been converted to panzergrenadier status was never chosen to act as a striking force on a major front.

The foreign SS divisions, with the exception of *Wiking* and *Nordland*, were all either too small or too poorly motivated to count for anything in events of the scale in which they found themselves involved. None of the western European SS units ever achieved much more than regimental strength, and, with whatever desperation they fought even until the end, regiments were the small change of strategy in a war decided between Army Groups. Most of the east European SS was riff-raff with the exception of the Latvian and Estonian divisions, which were fighting in the defence of their own homelands. The rest were contemptible or pathetic and did nothing to further the German war effort – indeed through their consumption of munitions which could have been better used by conventional formations, probably hindered it.

But the élite, *Leibstandarte*, *Reich*, *Totenkopf*, *Hohenstauffen*, *Frundsberg*, *Hitler Jugend* were without question divisions of the highest quality, greatly esteemed by the generals fortunate enough to have them under command, rightly feared by their enemies. Whether they were better than the divisions with whom they must be strictly equated – the best of the army panzer divisions – is imponderable. Indeed rather than compare the two categories it is probably more valid to view them as parts of a whole, the armoured spearhead of the Wehrmacht. In that spearhead, the élite Waffen SS divisions formed by 1943 an important proportion – nearly a quarter – and their performance and their outlook had become, by that stage of the war, more or less indistinguishable from the rest. This gave grounds for unease to Himmler, who complained in August 1941 that 'in

Hitler, Himmler and Henlein, leader of the Sudeten Germans

one SS division Wehrmacht ranks are used exclusively both on and off duty. Whether on duty or not and in all correspondence through the field post SS commanders will use only SS ranks'. (The SS had inherited its arcane titles of rank from the SA.) Another high SS official reported of Steiner, *Wiking's* commander, in 1942, that he was 'modelling himself mentally on the Wehrmacht' and if that were true of such a thorough-going SS man it is likely to have been true also of many others. Towards the end of war, however, it does seem probable that the élite Waffen SS divisions

overtook the army panzer divisions in quality, but only because they enjoyed preference in drafts of reinforcements and the supply of equipment.

One respect in which it is important to seek differences between the Waffen SS and the army is over the question of atrocities. The SS, in which was specifically included the Waffen SS, was, unlike the army, indicted as a criminal organisation at Nuremberg and both during and since the termination of those trials the German generals, and other representatives of the German army, have constantly striven to show that all atrocities committed in the field were the work of Himmler's men. They have not

shall in the near future be able to apportion blame fairly between one category of German soldier and another. It does seem, however, that more blameworthy incidents are attributable to the Wehrmacht than the generals would like to admit. They would of course wish to admit none but it would be impossible for them to deny that the Commissar Order (which enjoined the instant execution of all political commissars taken prisoner) applied equally to army and SS and was carried out by both, though by the latter with none of the reluctance admittably shown by some units of the former. It would also be difficult to deny, since army and SS troops were both employed on anti-partisan duty, that a proportion at least of the families and neighbours of partisans who were undoubtedly and deliberately killed in the course of such operations died at the hands of the army. And it would be very difficult to disprove that the deaths of some, probably many of the millions of Russian soldiers who died in captivity lost their lives through the callousness or neglect of their captors and that some Wehrmacht units at some times shot their captives out of hand.

That being said, it is nevertheless unarguable that the German army behaved in the west with marked correctness, while units of at least four of the divisions of the Waffen SS, *Totenkopf*, *Das Reich*, *Leibstandarte* and *Hitler Jugend* committed atrocities there, the first three on a major scale at Le Paradis, Oradour and Malmedy respectively. *Hitler Jugend's* misconduct is less well remembered though its commander, Kurt Meyer, was condemned to death for war crimes. The court established that units of his division, acting apparently with his approval, had shot sixty-four British and Canadian prisoners, many of whom were wounded, during the battle of Normandy. Meyer, the youngest officer of the general rank in the German armed forces, and

usually laid the responsibility on the Waffen SS itself but on that heterogeneous mass of security, police, anti-partisan and local volunteer troops which came under the command of Himmler's Higher SS and police leaders, in whom authority over the rear areas of the operational zones in the east was vested. But where combat soldiers have been unmistakably identified, the defenders of the army's reputation have always been quick to insist that they must have been members of the Waffen SS. What substance is there in this condemnation?

Since the scale and confusion of the fighting in the east defies accurate dissection, it seems unlikely that we

Left : Presentation of colours to the SS Heimwehr Danzig, 1939. This unit later became part of the Totenkopf division
Above : In Holland survivors show signs of strain

known as 'Panzermeyer' or 'Schnell-meyer' for his dash in action, had always served hitherto on the eastern front where presumably such practices were commonplace.

But besides incidental atrocities committed by combat formations of the Waffen SS, any assessment of its criminal character must take into account the presence in its order of battle of units which were criminal by nature and function. The best-known of these are the Dirlewanger and Kaminski brigades. Dirlewanger, a veteran Nazi with a past dubious even by the reckoning of the least fastidious of 'old party fighters', was commissioned in 1940 by his patron, Berger, the head of Himmler's recruiting office, to assume command of a unit of convicted poachers. The notion was that men of that stamp could far more usefully discharge their sentences hunting partisans than breaking stones and, when trained, they were shipped off to the eastern front to fight in the rear-area guerilla

war. Their behaviour on garrison duty at Cracow attracted such unfavourable notice that the unit was transferred to a less populated zone, and there the success of their methods in anti-partisan operations led to a second battalion being raised and put under Dirlewanger's command. In 1944 it, and another irregular SS unit, Kaminski's brigade of renegade Ukrainians, were sent to Obergruppenführer von dem Bach-Zelewski to help in the reduction of the Warsaw rising and their atrocious conduct in the city so outraged observers – even some who were members of the SS – that they prevailed upon Hitler to withdraw these units from the fighting. This was not the first time that SS units had committed atrocities in the city: the clearing of the Warsaw Ghetto in 1943 was carried out under the direction of Brigadeführer Stroop, by two battalions of SS recruits under training in the vicinity, with unimaginable brutality. The Jews possessed a few hundred revolvers with which to defend themselves against flame-throwers and field guns. Even so, Stroop collected and had handsomely bound a photographic record of the *Grossaktion* which he presented to Himmler. 'The dirty arrogant SS swine', General Jodl was to burst out

at Nuremberg 'Imagine writing a boastful seventy-five page report on a little murder expedition, when a major campaign fought by soldiers against a well-armed army takes only a few pages'.

Defendants of the Waffen SS have always argued that the crimes of the Dirlewanger and Kaminski brigades do not reflect on its honour because the two were never properly part of the organisation. Kaminski's units certainly seem to belong more properly to the host of east European volunteer security units raised under the aegis of the SS, rather than to its fighting branch proper, but it and Dirlewanger's brigade were nevertheless mustered on its strength and the latter eventually achieved the nominal status of a division (36th Waffen Grenadier). Nevertheless it is perhaps fair to give the Waffen SS the benefit of the doubt in these cases.

More significant in assessing its complicity in criminal activity is a reckoning of the proportion of concentration camp and security police personnel in its ranks. As we now know, the internal administration of the camps was in large measure turned over by the SS to selected prisoners; nevertheless the men of the *Totenkopfverbände* were intimately concerned in the camp's brutal and degrading regime, particularly in the early days, and it was they who went to form the complement of the original *Totenkopf* division. Other *Totenkopfstandarten* were employed in repressive duties, which often included deportation and extermination, before being embodied in the Waffen SS for front-line service. And there was throughout the war a constant coming and going between the concentration camp and field branches of the SS at almost every level. The rank and file of the field divisions of the SS

Von dem Bach Zelewski poses for propaganda photograph with wounded prisoners taken during the Warsaw uprising of September 1944

Himmler with Heydrich in the halcyon days

Hitler and his generals, 1936

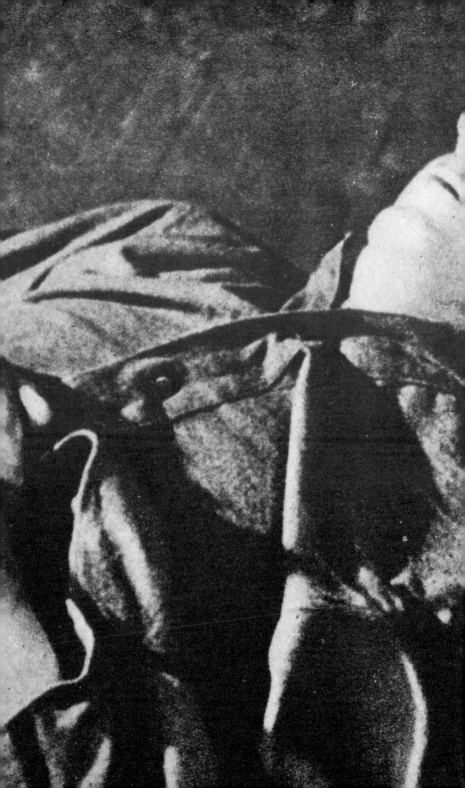

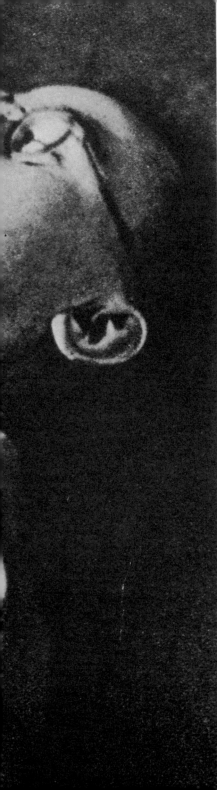

Himmler's body after his suicide in British captivity, 21st May 1945

must therefore have been well aware of the workings of the camp system and there is no record of their objecting to serving side by side with men so transferred.

It would therefore seem difficult to exempt the Waffen SS from the charges laid against it at Nuremberg, it being always understood that the verdict returned was held not to constitute proof of the guilt of individual members, many no doubt can honestly affirm that they were party to no sort of atrocity and knew of the extermination and concentration camp system only in a round-about and general way. Perhaps some knew not even that.

Nevertheless, the flavour of harshness, even of brutality hangs inexpungeably about the Waffen SS. However narrowly restricted is the list of 'true' SS divisions, and whatever extenuation is found for the excesses even they committed, Himmler's soldiers were not like other soldiers. It was not that they swore a different oath or wore a different uniform, but rather that they had opted for a different philosophy of war. The roots of that philosophy are many-branched. Some derive from the creed of the superman, propounded by that most unsympathetic of all German thinkers, Friedrich Nietzsche. Others were nurtured by epic myth and legend, of which German literature has so full a store, and by stories of the deeds of the heroes of German history, Frundsberg and Götz among them. Comradeship and its responsibilities were an important component of the SS philosophy, as was the ideal of youth itself, both stemming from the outlook of the German youth movement of the immediate pre- and post-Great War years. Perhaps most formative of all was the nihilistic tradition of the *Freikorps*, whose ghosts fought their last battle in the ruins of the Berlin Chancellery in April 1945.

The style of title conferred on the Waffen SS divisions varied, depending on its racial composition. Those composed of German volunteers were styled 'SS – Division'; those of 'racial' Germans or Germanic volunteers, 'SS – Freiwilligen – Division'; those of east Europeans, 'Division de Waffen SS'. In all cases the number (conferred in 1942) came first and the name last; where necessary, a national description was appended.

Name	Raised	Composition	Strength	Fate
1st SS Panzerdivision Leibstandarte Adolf Hitler	1933	German	successively a regiment, brigade and division	Capitulated 1945
2nd SS Panzerdivision Das Reich	1939	German	divisional	Capitulated 1945
3rd SS Panzerdivision Totenkopf	1940	German	divisional	Capitulated 1945
4th SS Polizei – Panzergrenadierdivision	1940	German	divisional	Capitulated 1945
5th SS Panzerdivision Wiking	late 1940	German/West European	divisional	Capitulated 1945
6th SS Gebirgsdivision Nord	late 1940	German	brigade, later divisional	Capitulated 1945
7th SS Freiwilligen-Gebirgsdivision Prinz Eugen	1942 1942	Racial Racial German from Yugoslavia	divisional divisional	Capitulated Capitulated 1945
8th SS Kavalleriedivision Florian Geyer	1942	German/racial German	divisional	Capitulated 1945
9th SS Panzerdivision Hohenstauffen	1943	German	divisional	Capitulated 1945
10th SS Panzerdivision Frundsberg	1943	German	divisional	Capitulated 1945

Waffen SS divisions

11th SS Freiwilligen-Panzergrenadierdivision Nordland	late 1942	German/West European	divisional	Capitulated 1945
12th SS Panzerdivision Hitler Jugend	1943	German	divisional	Capitulated 1945
13th Waffen-Gebirgsdivision der SS Handschar (kroatische Nr 1)	1943	Yugoslav Muslim	divisional	Disbanded 1944
14th Waffen-Grenadier-division der SS (galizische Nr 1)	1943	Ukrainian	divisional	Capitulated 1945
15th Waffen-Grenadier-division der SS (lettische Nr 1)	1943	Latvian/German	divisional	Capitulated 1945
16th SS Panzergrenadier-division Reichsführer SS	1943	German/racial German	divisional	Capitulated 1945
17th SS Panzergrenadier-division Götz von Berlichingen	1943	German/racial German	divisional	Capitulated 1945
18th SS Freiwilligen-Panzergrenadierdivision Horst Wessel	1944	German/racial German	divisional	Capitulated 1945
19th Waffen Grenadier-division der SS (lettische Nr 2)	1944	Latvian	divisional	Capitulated 1945
20th Waffen Grenadier-division der SS (estnische Nr 1)	1944	Estonian	divisional	Capitulated 1945
21st Waffen Gebirgsdivision der SS Skanderberg (albanische Nr 1)	1944	Albanian Muslin	never fully formed	Disbanded 1944
22nd SS Freiwilligen-Kavalleriedivision Maria Theresia	1944	Racial German/German	divisional	Capitulated 1945

Order of battle of

23rd Waffen Gebirgsdivision der SS Kama (kroatische Nr 2)	1944	Yugoslav Muslim	never fully formed	Disbanded 1944
(2) 23rd SS Freiwilligen-Panzerdivision Nederland	1945	Dutch	regimental	Capitulated 1945
24th Waffen Gebirgskarst jägerdivision der SS	1944	Italian/racial German	unknown	Dissolved 1945
25th Waffen Grenadier-division der SS Hunyadi (ungarische Nr 1)	late 1944	Hungarian	unknown	Disappeared
26th Waffen Grenadier-division der SS (ungarische Nr 2)	late 1944	Hungarian	unknown	Disappeared
27th SS Freiwilligen-Grenadierdivision Langemarck	1945	Flemish-Belgian	regimental	Capitulated 1945
28th SS Freiwilligen-Grenadierdivision Wallonien	1945	Walloon-Belgian	regimental	Capitulated 1945
29th Waffen Grenadier-division der SS (russische Nr 1)	1944	Russian	regimental	Transferred to the Vlasov Army 1944
(2) 29th Waffen Grenadier-division der SS (italische Nr 1)	1945	Italian	regimental	Disappeared 1945
30th Waffen Grenadier-division der SS (russische Nr 2)	1944	Russian	regimental	Transferred to the Vlasov Army, 1944
31st SS Freiwilligen-Panzerdivision Böhmen-Mähren	1945	German/racial German	regimental	Capitulated 1945
32nd SS Panzergrenadier-division 30 Januar	1945	German	regimental	Capitulated 1945

Waffen SS divisions

33rd Waffen Kavallerie-division der SS (ungarische Nr 3)	1945	Hungarian	regimental	Annihilated 1945
(2) 33rd Waffen Grenadier-division der SS Charlemagne (franzosische Nr 1)	1945	French	regimental	Annihilated Berlin 1945
34th SS Freiwilligen-Grenadierdivision Landstorm Nederland	1945	Dutch	regimental	Dissolved 1945
35th SS Polizei-Grenadierdivision	1945	German Policemen	regimental	Dissolved 1945
36th Waffen Grenadier-division der SS	1945	Originally Dirlewanger's Brigade	brigade	Capitulated 1945
37th SS Freiwilligen-Kavalleriedivision Lützow	1945	Racial German	regimental	Capitulated 1945
38th SS Panzergrenadier-division Nibelungen	1945	SS Officer cadets	regimental	Capitulated 1945

Notes
1. 23rd (2), 27th, 28th and 33rd (2) were originally 'Legions', belonging either to the SS or the army.
2. Most units numbered above 20 were of indifferent quality or under-strength.
3. Gebirgsdivision: mountain division; Grenadierdivision: infantry division; Panzergrenadierdivision: motorised infantry division.

Bibliography

The SS: Alibi of a Nation Gerald Reitlinger (Heinemann, London. Viking Press, New York)

The Final Solution Gerald Reitlinger (Heinemann, London. A S Barnes, Cranbury, NJ)

The House Built on Sand Gerald Reitlinger (Weidenfeld and Nicholson, London. Viking Press, New York)

Young Germany Walter Laqueur (Weidenfeld and Nicholson, London. Basic Books, New York)

Inside Hitler's Headquarters Walter Warlimont (Weidenfeld and Nicholson, London. Praeger, New York)

Barbarossa Alan Clark (Hutchinson, London. New American Library, New York)

Panzer Battles F W von Mellenthin (Cassell, London. University of Oklahoma Press, Oklahoma)

Parades and Politics at Vichy Robert Paxton (Princeton University Press, NJ)

Die Panzergrenadiere F M von Senger and Etterlin (Lehmanns Verlag, Munich. Adler's Foreign Books, New York)

Panzer Leader General Heinz Guderian (Michael Joseph, London. Ballantine Books, New York)

To Lose a Battle Alistaire Horne (Macmillan, London. Little, Boston)

Hitler, a Study in Tyranny Alan Bullock (Oldham, London. Harper and Row, New York)

The Ardennes Hugh M Cole (US Army Official History, Washington)

Politics of the Prussian Army Gordon Craig (Oxford University Press, London and New York)

Reichswehr and Politics F L Carsten (Oxford University Press, London and New York)

The Nemesis of Power Sir John Wheeler-Bennet (Macmillan, London. Viking Press, New York)

German Army and the Nazi Party R J O'Neill (Corgi, London. Heineman, New York)

The Rise and Fall of the Third Reich W L Shirer (Pan Books, London. Fawcett World Library, Greenwich, Connecticut)

War in France and Flanders L F Ellis (HMSO, London)

Waffen SS George S Stein (Oxford University Press, London. Cornell University Press, New York)